Old-Time
Dude Ranches Out West

Waiting for the Wrangler. (Photo by Harrison R. Crandall, from the Crandall Family collection)

OLD-TIME DUDE RANCHES OUT WEST

ELIZABETH CLAIR FLOOD

GIBBS·SMITH PUBLISHER

SALT LAKE CITY

For my friend Adam,

who taught me

to be courageous.

Welcome to the Tetons. (Photo by Harrison R. Crandall, from the Crandall Family collection)

First edition
97 96 95   5 4 3 2 1

Design by J. Scott Knudsen, Park City, Utah
Front cover art from *Dude Ranches Out West,* an early
Union Pacific Railroad brochure
Graphic and line art throughout was reproduced with permission from brochures
provided by various dude ranches.
Printed and bound in Hong Kong

Library of Congress Cataloging-in-Publication Data
Flood Elizabeth Clair, 1967–
    Old-time dude ranches out West/by Elizabeth Clair Flood.—1st ed.
        p.   cm.
    ISBN 0-87905-668-1 (pb)
    1. Dude ranches—West (U.S.) 2. Dude ranches—West (U.S.)—History. I Title.
GV198.96.W47F56   1994
796.56'0978—dc20

Contents

Dudeens sport their finest in western wear at the Pitchfork Ranch, circa 1940. Established in 1878 in the valley of the Greybull River in northwestern Wyoming, the Pitchfork is one of the state's oldest ranches. Its dude business closed in 1946. (Photo by Charles J. Belden, courtesy the Belden Museum, Meeteetse, WY)

Acknowledgments

This project was possible because Gibbs Smith dared to dream and my editor Madge Baird reined in two romantics and gave the project some form.

On the trail I met a crew of passionate folks, who imparted compelling information and stories about dude country. Brian Lebel of Old West Antiques in Cody, Wyoming, contributed invaluable knowledge, enthusiasm, and the majority of the dude memorabilia featured.

Elmer Dietrich of Big Timber, Montana, Senia Hart of Red Lodge, Montana, and Virginia Huidekoper of Jackson, Wyoming, also contributed a handful of old brochures and historical items I couldn't have done without. Thanks, of course, to my friend Tim Sandlin, who encouraged me to write.

I was helped considerably by the following organizations: Teton County Historical Society, The Western Heritage Center, King Ropes, The Belden Museum, The Library of Congress, University of Wyoming, The Dude Ranchers Association, and the Colorado Dude Ranchers Association. Jean Kilgore's book *Ranch Vacations* was an important resource, and Custom Color Lab of Jackson is responsible for making the first-class prints from original photos, used predominately throughout the book. Both Christine Watkins, who hand tinted the photographs, and Scott Knudsen, who designed the book, helped to create its romantic style.

While I can't list every dude rancher, I am deeply grateful to them for inviting me into their homes, sharing with me their photographs, stories and love for the business. I'm indebted to David Dominick for providing me with a pack-trip experience I'll never forget; Margi Schroth for inviting me on one of the most memorable rides and for giving me permission to use her William Elling Gollings illustrations; and to all the dude ponies who carried me into the backcountry.

Other folks who shared important dude memories and information include Margo and Cal Todd, Don and Dorothy King, Lili and Jack Turnell, Jack and Margaret Huyler, Mrs. Dornan, Michael Enright, Bob Rudd, Olie Riniker, Bo and Anna Polk, Emily Oliver, Hal Johnson, Ellen Mettler, Pam and John Mortensen, Fred Wyle, Cathy Lingard, Fred and Alvie Norris, and Emily Stevens. I was thrilled to meet Quita and Herb Pownell and Nancy and Chuck Cooper, who gave permission to use Harrison R. Crandall's photographs.

Throughout my four years in Wyoming and on the cowboy circuit, I have met a gang of western fanatics, who I lean on all the time for friendship, advice and good laughs. These folks include Milo and Teddi Marks, Sandy and Terry Winchell, Robert Hartman of *Cowboys and Indians* magazine, Ann Wilson of *West* magazine, Ray Thurston, Jerry Jordan, Jonathan Foote, Vicky Zwiefel, Julianne and Bruce Bartlett, and all my friends at the *Jackson Hole News*. Of course, I'm grateful to my parents and two sisters, Karin and Christina, for their love and support.

Introduction

As early as the 1880s, adventure-hungry easterners escaped the civilized grip of their society and traveled to the wild-'n'-woolly West in search of a ranch experience. The promise of roughing it in the wild, sleeping in the mountains under a canopy of stars, and living like the cowboys did drew these turn-of-the-century sophisticates to the Far West.

After arriving via the Union Pacific Railroad, and later in their own Model Ts, young eastern women changed into cowgirl garb and fell head-over-heels in love with roughnecks, while the men tramped into the wilderness looking for grizzly bear. These early guests with visions of rugged ranch living were the first species of a new western breed—the dude.

In the early days a *dude* was usually an easterner with a social-register listing. Other variations on the word included *dudeen*, describing a lady, or *dudette*, meaning a child or a lady smitten by a cowboy. The word "dude" was not pejorative; it was originally used to describe a guest who was not from the West and who paid to stay on a western ranch or for the services of a guide.

The dude ranch offered a traveler an experience chock-full of western fantasy. At the turn of the century and throughout dude ranching's heyday in the 1920s, the western ranch was as exotic a destination as the African wilderness. Traveling by train across the country or winding over rugged passes in a surrey or on horseback was difficult. One of the most flamboyant and undaunted of these early dudes was Teddy Roosevelt, who thrived on sleeping in the rain and mingling with cowboys and desperadoes.

As many ranchers have said, dude ranching started as a party among friends. When entertaining friends became expensive, families charged their frequent guests. Cattle ranchers often took in guests to supplement their income. Other travelers arrived at the depot in hope of finding a native guide to take them on a pack trip or hunting. Throughout Montana, Wyoming, and Colorado a few entrepreneurs set up hunting camps to entice tourists to the adventure-laden West.

Soon pack-trip outfits developed into dude operations and hunting camps expanded to accommodate women and children as well as men.

Many historians pinpoint the beginning of dude ranching as 1882, when Bert Rumsey of Buffalo, New York, wanted to

pay Howard, Alden, and Willis Eaton to stay at their Custer Trail cattle ranch in Medora, North Dakota. "I'm having a good time. I need the outdoor life. I don't want to go home. I've got plenty of money and I'd consider it a favor if you'd let me stay awhile and pay something each week for my board and the use of a horse," Rumsey told Howard Eaton. Rumsey signed the Eatons' guest register and paid $10 a week for a ranch experience, and the dude-ranch business began.

Other ranches were quick to follow the Eatons' early lead. Dick Randall—nick-named the father of dude ranching in Montana—was in the dude business by 1887. He had a small string of pack horses and, amongst many other odd jobs, guided hunters such as Owen Wister, author of

Where East Meets West. **(Photo by Harrison R. Crandall, from the Crandall Family collection)**

Top: Dudes racing toward Eatons' Ranch, 1918. (Photo courtesy Norina Shields)

The Virginian, Hartley Dodge of Remington Arms, railroad magnate Henry Villard, writer Philip Ashton Rollins, and Theodore Roosevelt. Many other Montana ranches soon sprang up.

Dude ranching spread into northern Wyoming after the Burlington Railroad reached Cody in 1903. That same year the road to the east entrance of Yellowstone park was opened, and William F. Cody's hunting lodges—the Irma Hotel, Wapiti Lodge, and Pahaska Tepee—attracted tourists west. In the midst of this early stampede, Tex Holme set up tents and a lodge at an 1898 stage stop outside of Yellowstone. The lodge served as an overnight stop for Yellowstone travelers.

One of the most significant ranches in this area was the Valley Ranch, owned by Larry Larom. A Princeton man raised on Park Avenue, Larom started the Valley Ranch in 1915 with Winthrop Brooks, a friend from Yale and the future president of Brooks Brothers' Clothier in New York. Under Larry and Win, the place developed into a posh club for their eastern friends. The two even ran Pullman cars and a diner on trains from New York to Cody. Larry also ran a prestigious prep school for boys at the ranch.

Dude ranching developed early in Colorado as well. In 1886, Mr. and Mrs. Campton opened a resort in St. Cloud in Larimer County called Campton's Hotel and Resort. Here well-to-do travelers enjoyed elegant accommodations and fresh mountain air. In 1890, Griff Evans and Abner Sprague in the Estes Park area were

High fashion at the Valley Ranch, 1940. (Photo by Charles J. Belden, courtesy The Belden Museum, Meeteetse, WY)

taking guests. On the western side of the Continental Divide, Squeaky Bob Wheeler started a dude ranch. Farther south and west in Colorado another ranch, owned by Lizzy Sullivan, began.

In Jackson Hole, Wyoming, dude ranching developed later, as it was difficult to settle the valley, noted for its long, cold winters and short summers. The first ranch was the JY, owned by Lou Joy and Struthers Burt in 1908. The second

Interior of a JY Ranch cabin. (Photo courtesy Virginia Huidekoper)

Above: A cowboy quenches his thirst at the Pitchfork Ranch. (Photo by Charles J. Belden, courtesy The Belden Museum, Meeteetse, WY.)

ranch to develop was Struthers Burt's famous Bar BC in 1912. Others, such as the White Grass, the Bear Paw, Triangle X, the R Lazy S, the Elbo, the Half Moon, and a slew of smaller ones from the STS to the Dude-For-A-Day, were soon to pop up. Add to this sudden growth the dramatic

Right: One of the majestic lodges of Glacier National Park. (Photo courtesy Norina Shields)

landscape and the charisma of the ranchers, and dude ranching in the Jackson Hole area was soon brimming with glamour and romance.

Princeton graduate and Philadelphia native Struthers Burt was responsible for inviting many of the wealthy travelers to the Jackson Hole valley. Several old-timers remember the glitter of the dance halls, riding to other ranches for late-night parties, and gambling at the Cowboy Bar.

While dude ranching developed as a result of these early charismatic leaders, their ranches, and their extensive eastern connections, the railroad campaign also made a significant impact on the industry. The railroads promoted Glacier and Yellowstone parks and the ranches in the vicinity. They promised prospective dudes great scenery and simple comforts in dude-ranch country.

In 1913, Louis W. Hill, president of the Great Northern Railway, encouraged passengers to visit Glacier National Park in northern Montana with his catchy slogan "See America First." To entice eastern tenderfeet to the Wild West, Hill built two majestic log lodges, smaller backcountry chalets, and a far-flung network of trails.

The Burlington Northern and Union Pacific were big promoters of dude travel. The railroad companies sent out brochures—more like small books—full of photos, sophisticated graphics and information to entice romantics to the wild. Often railroad representatives would show up at a ranch and ask the ranch if they wanted to accept dudes. If the owners agreed, the railroad company would take care of all the advertising. Professional photographers and reporters were sent out west to capture the fantasy.

As numerous ranches were established, the dude ranchers felt a need to meet and discuss how they could promote the business as a whole. In 1926, the group met at

Above: A brave dude tries his style at calf riding. (Photo by Stan Kershaw, courtesy Brian Lebel)

Right: Fly-fishing on the Pitchfork River. (Photo by Charles J. Belden, courtesy The Belden Museum, Meeteetse, WY)

Right: Wranglers and dudes sing away the hours before bedtime. (Photo by Stan Kershaw, courtesy Brian Lebel.)

Far right: A wrangler gives the guests a lesson in tying knots. (Photo by Charles J. Belden, courtesy The Belden Museum, Meeteetse, WY)

the Bozeman Hotel in Bozeman, Montana. Larry Larom was elected president of The Dude Ranchers' Association. The ranchers eventually developed a set of rules: Guests must stay at least a week. They shouldn't solicit business from the road. Riding is the main activity. And a ranch must not sell alcoholic beverages.

With all this attention to the new industry, dude ranching exploded in the 1920s, enjoying a heyday unmatched in any other era. Because of the war, people accustomed to European travel now explored their own country. Like Paris, the West was a haven for artists and a more unconventional crowd. Rules were few, freedom plenty. And the juxtaposition of debutantes and cowpunchers, champagne and horse manure, polo and poker games created an exotic and classless environment where anything went.

What went on at a dude ranch? For the most part, these ranches were difficult to get to and isolated. Cabins were simple, without electricity or running water. A metal bucket was provided for bathing, and the privy was usually a short jaunt across the sage.

On the early dude ranch, the host, several wranglers, a cabin girl or maid, and that all-important person—the cook—catered to the needs of about twenty to thirty guests.

Although people insisted, and still insist, that the term *dude* is not an insult, there is no question that westerners did poke a little fun at the green easterner upon arrival. "They were so gullible, they would believe anything," says Bob Kranenberg, a hand at the Square G Ranch in Wyoming during the 1930s and 1940s. "We had to straighten some of them out." Bob remembers moving the outhouse and watching a helpless dude searching for the privy in the midst of a snowstorm. He also remembers a wrangler friend telling him he had spooked his dudes

with his own mountain lion call. The wrangler told one particularly gullible city dweller that when a mountain lion picks up your scent, you are a goner. The only way to avoid his attack was to strip down and coat yourself with bacon grease. Without hesitation, the tenderfoot followed instructions.

A dude ranch was always much more than a summer hotel. From the early days these ranches that succeeded were the ones that combined eastern thinking and clientele with western common sense and expertise. A dude rancher had to be well versed in both the eastern and western lifestyles for his ranch to run smoothly. Struthers Burt knew the ingredients: "If you wish to sum up the dude-business in a sentence, it consists in giving people homemade bedsteads but forty-pound mattresses."

Dude business dropped off a bit in the thirties as a result of the depression, and then continued to grow throughout the forties and fifties. A slew of new dude ranches opened in the sixties as people's interest in the West soared. Today, with the overwhelming worldwide interest in the West, dude ranches are booked solid, and a few ranchers speculate that they are in the midst of another heyday.

Few ranches, however, are able to retain the old-time feeling as guests demand more luxuries and large ranches become increasingly difficult to maintain. And many ranches have succumbed to the glitz and glamour of a more resortlike operation. Ranches are also trying to accommodate the tourist who wants to see a lot in a short amount of time rather than the early traveler who stayed for months.

But the old-time dude ranch was an exciting, romantic, and truly American tradition. Unlike today, guests adopted the nickname "dude" or "dudeen." As one early dude rancher from the East said proudly,

"You are a dude 'til you die." For many, the title conveyed a romantic ranking.

Out West the dude-ranch legacy still lingers as a handful of ranchers preserve a way of life and an important tradition. *Dude Ranches Out West* highlights the working ranch as well as the dude ranch. The former raises cattle and takes care of dudes, while the latter is strictly a dude dwelling. As much as possible, the ranches featured in this book started at the turn of the century or in the twenties and are still run today by the same family. They offer guests a rustic experience in the West: riding is the main activity; food is homemade; guests must stay at least a week; and everyone is treated like an old friend in a family's home.

Top: Dudes leave a chapel near the Bear Paw Ranch, Jackson Hole, Wyoming. (Photo courtesy Jack Huyler.)

Bottom: Supper, a pot of cowboy coffee and a campfire—what could be more romantic? (Photo by Stan Kershaw, courtesy Brian Lebel.)

Bar Lazy

P.O. BOX N
PARSHALL, COLORADO 80468

In 1904 fishermen laden with rods, flies, and wicker creels headed for Mr. and Mrs. Ferguson's Buckhorn Lodge. Located on the Colorado River just northwest of Denver, the lodge was a hot spot for the passionate angler. For the most part, these guests were dry dudes, or nonpaying guests.

In 1911 Mr. and Mrs. Messiter opened the lodge to paying guests. The main attraction was still the rainbow trout. High tea was served at 4:00 in the afternoon and dinner at 8:00 P.M. Polo matches were held on the grounds. And as with most ranches, references were required of new guests. In these early years, the staff was not allowed to mingle with guests. The ranch was also noted to have a good and reliable chef, a real novelty in those days.

Today the Buckhorn Lodge, now called the Bar Lazy J, is considered the oldest operating guest ranch in the state. While fishing is still a large draw, guests today have a more diverse palette of interests, say

Little dudes not only learn to ride like cowboys but to dance like them too. (Photo courtesy Bar Lazy J)

owners Larry and Barbara Harmon, who bought the place in 1987. The ranch is proud of its first-class fishing, riding operation, and kids' program.

The ranch has two-thirds of a mile of private Colorado River access where only Bar Lazy J fishing dudes are allowed, except for sunbathers who coach from the grassy shores. At the beginning of a week at the ranch, Jerry Craig, the old man of the river, meets guests and shares his knowledge. On request, he takes dudes afield to other fishing holes. And for young cowpokes, the ranch has stocked a fishing pond that is fed by natural springs.

Like the angling program, the horseback rides accommodate all abilities—slow, medium, and fast. Two rides go out a day, so guests can enjoy open spaces carpeted with sagebrush and hillsides covered with aspen. Often dudes spot deer and antelope on the trail that winds through the Arapaho National Forest and land owned by the Bureau of Land

Dudes enjoy a hayride at the Bar Lazy J. (Photo courtesy Bar Lazy J)

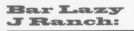

Early anglers brave the cold for some ice fishing. (Photo courtesy Bar Lazy J)

Bar Lazy J Ranch:

(303) 725–3437
Season: June–mid-September
Rates weekly: $965 adults,
    $300–800 children
Special activities: Fly-fishing
Airport: Denver
Guest capacity: 38
    Special children's program
    for ages 3–8

Management and the Colorado State Division of Wildlife.

As a result of personal care extended to guests, families come back year after year. "It's like old-home week," says Barbara. When the dinner bell rings everyone comes running. "Kids usually gobble their food then are out the door to play with the kittens, throw rocks in the river, or participate in our special activities."

At the Bar Lazy J, the Harmons have developed a strong children's program that enables kids and adults to enjoy their own adventures. There are two counselors for children ages three to nine. Preteens have the run of the ranch. Activities include hiking, fishing, square dancing, and riding instruction, in addition to many games and a well-equipped play area.

Recipe from the Bar Lazy J

ZUCCHINI BREAD

3 eggs
2 cups sugar
1 cup vegetable oil
1 Tbsp. vanilla
2 cups zucchini, coarsely grated & loosely packed
2 cups sifted flour
1 Tbsp. cinnamon
1 tsp. salt
2 tsp. baking powder
1 cup chopped nuts (not too fine)

Beat eggs until frothy. Beat in sugar, oil, and vanilla. Stir in zucchini. Stir in dry ingredients. Fold in nuts. Pour into two oiled and floured loaf pans. Bake at 350° for 50–60 minutes, until a toothpick inserted in the middle comes out clean.

The Buckhorn Lodge was noted for having good food and a reliable cook. Tea was served every afternoon. (Photo courtesy Bar Lazy J)

The Buckhorn
Lodge, 1916. (Photo
courtesy Bar Lazy J)

Mr. Messiter enjoys
a quiet moment in
front of a warm fire.
(Photo courtesy Bar
Lazy J)

The Bar Lazy J was
a retreat for the
well-to-do at the
turn of the century.
(Photo courtesy Bar
Lazy J)

Cherokee Park

P.O. BOX 97
LIVERMORE, COLORADO 80536

As early as 1886, the West was considered a healthful retreat for the wealthy. In that year, Mr. and Mrs. Campton opened Campton's Hotel and Resort at St. Cloud in Larimer County, where guests had access to nearly five thousand acres of undeveloped land. Elegant accommodations were provided in one of thirty hotel rooms or twenty-two cottages.

The Camptons established the place as an "ideal retreat for health and restfulness." As a 1907 brochure proclaimed, "Within the house one finds rest, peace, and comfort; tables bountifully supplied with seasonable, well-prepared creature comforts; baths, and beds which invite balmy sleep, Nature's sweet restorer."

The Camptons offered lawn tennis, croquet, and Ping-Pong. "Fine riding and driving horses, carriage, mountain wagons, burros for the children and picnic parties are kept for hire." There was also a dance pavilion on the property, where guests enjoyed waltzing to an orchestra and lively square dances.

One of the greatest attractions at Campton's Hotel and Resort was a hot spring. Hotel guests and other visitors traveled miles to soak in what was believed to be "pure, life-giving water." The water was also described as possessing "special curative properties for many ailments, and is looked upon as an interposition of Divine Providence in behalf of the afflicted." Barrels of this water were carried away every season for use in Fort Collins, Laramie, and Cheyenne.

Many of the old buildings still exist and a collection of early furniture, western memorabilia, and historic photos invite the guest to step back in time and enjoy a past era. Today, Eli and B Elfland are the hosts at Campton's place, now Cherokee Park Ranch.

Frank Miller performing at the ranch circa 1940s. Miller, a notorious figure in Larimer County history, was a sharpshooter who traveled around performing in many rodeos and shows. He owned some of the cabins on the ranch. (Photo courtesy Fort Collins Public Library)

Facing page: Dudette bathing beauties. (Photo courtesy Fort Collins Public Library)

Cherokee Ranch:

(800) 628–0949
Season: May–September
Rates weekly: July and August:
adults $1,100, 6–12 $850,
3–5 $700, under 3 $200; Low
season (May, June, September):
adults $900, 6–12 $775, 3–5
$700, under 3 $200
Special activities: Pack trips, fly-
fishing, white-water trips,
swimming
Airport: Denver
Guest capacity: 35

Cherokee Park offers riding as the main activity, but guests also shoot whitewater in rafts, fly-fish on the north fork of the Cache La Poudre River, hike, sightsee, trapshoot and try their hand at an old-time black-powder shoot. In the evenings the ranch offers hayrides, square dances, and sing-alongs.

Still in their twenties, the Elflands are part of a growing group of young dude ranchers. "What is special about the ranch for us and the guests are the people," B says. In this environment, participating in unfamiliar activities, guests loosen up and in most cases the best of their personality shines. And some of the strongest friendships are made.

As at many other ranches, the guests leave with a lump in their throat and tears in their eyes. Numerous guests look for-

A little guest shows appreciation for her dude pony. Photo Courtesy Cherokee Park Ranch)

CHEROKEE P

Your Dude Pony

"The dude horse or dude pony, as it is called in this connection, is the breath of life of the dude ranch," wrote Lawrence B. Smith in his book *Dude Ranches and Ponies* (Coward McCann, 1936). A horse is an essential companion for a dude who wants to travel western trails.

For the most part dude ponies don't have pedigrees. A good dude rancher, however, handpicks each one. They must be plumb gentle, reliable, strong, approximately fifteen hands tall, and—believe it or not—good-looking.

"No dude likes to be mounted on a rough, ugly looking brute, no matter how good a horse may be," wrote Lawrence R. Borne in his book *Dude Ranching: A Complete History*. "He likes a good looking quad, and color helps a lot; that is why pinto ponies are so popular as dude ponies."

A dude ranch usually has anywhere between thirty and a hundred horses, and each one has a name. "We name our horses after things around here, or sometimes they just earn their names," B Elfland said about the Cherokee Park horses. The string includes Banjo, Maverick, Cowboy, Injun, Amber, and Rugby, among others. Stubbs at Cherokee Park got his name because the tips of his ears froze off; Shamrock has an unusual coat of green; and Mom—well, everyone has a Mom on the string.

ward to returning, many booking the same cabin as well as requesting their same trusty steed. Friendships made continue to grow as many guests return during the same weeks to familiar faces, laughter, and memories. "It's always rewarding to have kids say this is the greatest vacation they have ever had—even better than Disney World," Eli says. "Half the kids want to pack their horses in their suitcases."

Right: Fly-fishing has become a popular pastime at Cherokee Park Ranch. (Photo courtesy Cherokee Park Ranch.)

Below: Dudes lined up in front of the Cherokee Park lodge, circa 1940s. (Photo courtesy Fort Collins Public Library)

UDE RANCH   MILLER

Circle Z

A Circle Z wrangler thought he had seen it all, until the Smith family arrived in the late 1930s. Zigzagging through the meadows on horseback, past mesquite and Arizona walnut trees, the family waved their butterfly nets in pursuit of the illusive insects. The family also took note of the myriad of wildflowers and numerous cacti and captured a few lizards to take back to the ranch. They were always partial to a small patch of rare blue star flowers, commonly called Jesus Tears, found in Flux Canyon along the riverbed and floodplains.

As a child, Lucia Smith Nash looked forward to returning to her favorite spots on the ranch. "It was such fun to revisit my favorite canyons, wildflowers, and picnic spots," she says. Of course, she paid a special visit to her tiny blue star flowers on each occasion.

While dude ranching developed in the northern Rocky Mountain region, Arizona quickly became a place for dude ranchers and wranglers in the winter off-season. The Circle Z is surrounded by 6,000 acres of undeveloped land. Nestled in the foothills of the Patagonia Mountains in southern Arizona, it is one of the oldest dude ranches in the state. It was started in 1926 by Lee George Zinsmeister. An early brochure claimed the ranch was "a place where people who are accustomed to the very best service, comfortable living conditions and a love for the out-of-doors, can spend their vacation or take a rest away from the hustle and turmoil of fashionable resorts and enjoy the novel experience of the life on a big cattle ranch without many discomforts which are usually and necessarily forced on a Ranch Guest."

The hub of the Circle Z is an adobe lodge. Inside, a warm fire, shelves stacked with books, and comfy furniture invite guests to get

Early guests in riding clothes. (Photo courtesy Circle Z Ranch)

A young cowboy in training. Below: A posse of dudes hits the trail. (Photo by Ray Manley, courtesy Circle Z Ranch)

Don Farrell and his stallion El Sultan provided endless hours of entertainment for dudes in the 1930s and '40s. (Photo courtesy Circle Z Ranch)

References Required

"**C**ircle 'Z' Ranch is truly a place of personal service, where the needs, comforts and pleasures of the individual guest are always foremost in thought. It is a place for new life, where the conventions of the outside world are laid aside, where one can refresh spirit, body and mind unconsciously. A place that will be left with regrets and with always a promise to return.

"The greatest care is used in the selection of guests, and references are requested from those anticipating a visit with us. In return the Zinsmeister Ranch Company will be pleased to reciprocate. This is for our mutual protection."

—*From a 1928 Circle Z guest brochure. The ranch no longer requires references.*

cozy. Scattered nearby are a group of private cottages with baths and a cantina where guests mingle before dinner.

In the 1970s, when Lucia Nash and her husband found out there was a plan afoot to develop their beloved riding area, they took a bold step and in 1972 purchased the land surrounding the ranch. Two years later they became owners of the ranch. Everyone was thankful, from the vermilion fly catcher to javelinas to dudes.

"Saving that land from being developed and saving the ranch and the kind of values it stands for—courteousness, pride in your work, western hospitality, respect for the land—was the greatest feeling. These ranch values were the same values my family lived by," Lucia says.

Once Lee and Helen Zinsmeister's adobe home, this building is now the main lodge, where guests enjoy family-style dinners and cozy evenings by the fire. (Photo courtesy Circle Z Ranch)

The Circle Z has always provided a first-rate string of sure-footed dude ponies. (Photo courtesy Circle Z Ranch)

Circle Z riders often visited Patagonia, in the heart of cattle-ranching country. It is one of the few authentic frontier towns left today. (Photo courtesy Circle Z Ranch)

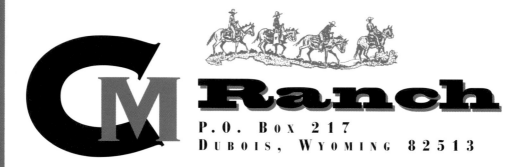

CM Ranch

P.O. Box 217
Dubois, Wyoming 82513

Upper right: A handsome wrangler poses for the girls. "Of course, all the girls were crazy about the cowboys. That's just a fact of life," says Alice Shoemaker. (Photo courtesy CM Ranch)

A Pennsylvania family arrives at the CM Ranch in hope of escaping the fast-paced life of sirens, fax machines, and gin-and-tonic cocktail parties. Once at the ranch, they want to don cowboy hats and ride into the mountains. To their dismay, they aren't allowed to ride unsupervised. "No one rides without a wrangler," says manager and part owner Peter Petersen. Grumbling ricochets throughout the lodge.

"When people find out how our rides are structured, though, they're glad to have a guide along," Pete says. Guests learn about the geology of the area, discuss ranching issues, listen to stories, and experience a westerner's way of thinking. "On a morning ride guests pass rocks representing 700 million years every mile. It would be an empty experience to ride by with idle chatter," says Pete, a knowledgeable geologist.

"We ride in small groups and, more

A CM Ranch girl. (Photo courtesy CM Ranch)

often than not, friendships are built during these rides," Pete says. "I don't like the word *bonding*, but when people ride together for a week, they get a very special feeling. You almost hate to take your guests' money at the end."

Charles Cornell Moore, founder of the ranch, was born in 1880. His father owned the Fort Washakie trading post on the Shoshone-Arapaho Indian Reservation, so Charlie grew up among Indians, trappers, cowboys, and hunters. In his teens, Charlie was sent to a prep school in New Jersey. Following his education, he wrangled and rode in Buffalo Bill's Wild West Show for a stint, then earned a law degree and practiced for a while. Finally he returned to his home in Wyoming.

In 1907 Moore opened the first camp for boys in the Rocky Mountains. "To the shut-in city boy, worn from the long winter's schoolwork and confinement, several weeks

CM Ranch:

(307) 455–2331
Season: Mid-June to end of August
Rates: On request
Special activities: Pack trips, swimming, fly-fishing
Airport: Jackson Hole or Riverton
Guest capacity: 55
  Full-time babysitter

The CM Ranch is located at the mouth of Jackey's Fork, a river named after Charlie Moore's father. The ranch is on the east slope of the main range of the Rocky Mountains, just across the Continental Divide from Jackson Hole and southeast of Yellowstone. This photograph was the cover of a ranch brochure in the 1920s. (Photo courtesy CM Ranch)

Boys' Camps

Charlie Moore's camp for boys. (Photo courtesy CM Ranch)

Charles Moore believed children could benefit from an outdoors education and launched the first Rocky Mountain boys' camp in 1907. The camp opened July 1 and ended mid-August. Boys took pack trips into Yellowstone National Park and around Jackson Hole country. They learned to camp, fish, fend for themselves in the wilderness and, of course, ride.

The purpose of the camp was to provide wealthy young men with an outdoor experience, "where they may have all the benefits and pleasures of ranch life, with the additional advantage of wholesome supervision of men of culture and education," wrote Moore. By the end of the two-month stint, boys exhibited extraordinary growth and maturity—some finding it difficult to slip back into their city clothes and return east.

An early brochure made very clear that only boys from upper-class families were accepted to the program: "References satisfactory to the Director must be furnished. The right is reserved to reject any application or to sever any boy's connection with the camp when his influence is deemed harmful." Many of the boys attended the Ivy League schools, such as Harvard, Yale, and Princeton.

Because parents insisted on visiting their children, Moore was prompted to buy some land in 1920 and build a few cabins to accommodate his visitors, while trying to maintain the camp. These parents were Moore's first dudes. Soon the dude business became so overwhelming, Moore was forced to abandon his pack trips for boys and focus on accommodating his summer revelers.

In the twenties, however, Moore did start a winter school for boys, which emphasized studying in the morning and outdoor activities in the afternoon. His brochure read: "A year or more of this healthful, active out-of-door life for the growing boy is of inestimable value and benefit." Apparently, the school was not a long-lasting success.

Just to the north, Larry Larom of the Valley Ranch also started summer camps for boys and girls, and a four-year preparatory school for boys, which enjoyed popularity for twelve years. With the advent of the depression, the school was closed.

of 'roughing it' in the interesting surroundings and under the favorable climate conditions of the Rockies is of lasting benefit and pleasure," wrote Moore in an early brochure.

For many dudes it is the character of the dude rancher that makes their stay worthwhile. In 1952, the CM was sold to Alice and Les Shoemaker, who had worked for Charlie. Their daughter, Leslie, remembers Charlie Moore's presence fondly. "He used to read the *Wall Street Journal* at the breakfast table. And he was very formal, distinguished and stern—except when he smiled." Charles Moore attracted a loyal clientele; the Shoemakers did as well. And now the Petersens are making lasting friendships with dudes that spawn repeat visits.

(Brochure courtesy Elmer Dietrich)

Left: Dudes gather on the fence to watch local cowboys compete in the weekly CM rodeo. In the early days, dudes participated in their own rodeo—a gymkhana featuring events such as pole bending and egg and water races. "It was just chaos," recalls Leslie Petersen. (Photo courtesy CM Ranch)

Below: The cabins at Simpson Lake, a National Historic Register site, have been a retreat for CM guests since the early days. Before owning the ranch, Alice Shoemaker used to cook for dudes at the Simpson cabins. Dudes would ride to the cabins, enjoy a hearty meal, spend the night, and take day trips to the Continental Divide. "Guests stayed up there about three or four days. That was about as long as people wanted to go without a shower," Alice remembers. (Photo courtesy CM Ranch)

Darwin Ranch

P.O. Box 511
Jackson, Wyoming 83001

Facing Page: Loring Woodman's first guest in 1965 takes in the view. (Photo courtesy Loring Woodman)

Inset: The Darwin Ranch is one of several that offer winter experiences for guests. (Photo courtesy Loring Woodman)

The directions said, "Meet at the green stake at 10 A.M."

Looking on the map at rugged terrain surrounded by the jagged peaks of the Gros Ventre and the Wind River Mountain ranges, it looked as though finding a green stake in this valley would be as unlikely as finding a bow tie in a cowboy's war bag.

"Take the Union Pass Road in from Dubois. The road will bear right after 11.5 miles, then left, then approximately 3 miles later take a right across Fish Creek. When you come to a cattle guard some 9.6 miles later, go straight. Bear left at Mosquito Lake. Go straight over the next cattle guard. Then 2.7 miles later a *faint*, barely used road comes in from the left. Meet there."

The total drive takes almost two hours from Dubois, Wyoming. Bumping along on a dirt road riddled with potholes, traversing fields of sage, cow pastures, and streams, I constantly wondered if I was going the right way. The last line of the directions was anything but comforting.

"We have placed a thin green metal fence post in the ground as a marker at the junction where we will pick you up, but since this is the sort of thing that can get borrowed or removed, don't count on it 100 percent."

Finding the green stake was actually the easy part of the trek into the Darwin Ranch. "Leave your car here, grab your stuff, and hop into the Suburban," said Loring Woodman, owner of the ranch.

From the pickup point, it was still thirty minutes or more to the ranch. We bumped and dipped and slid and forded deep puddles as we sank deeper and deeper into the wilderness.

The first owner of the property was a trapper named Fred Dorwin (not Darwin—the ranch later got its name as a result of a typographical error). Rumor has it that Dorwin had been a Rough Rider with Teddy Roosevelt, who granted him the land. Loring's father purchased the property in 1964, and Loring became a dude rancher, taking his first guests that

Darwin Ranch:

(307) 733–0410
Season: Summer: June
18–September 25;
Hunting: September
1–November 1;
Winter: open on
demand for groups of
6 or more
Rates daily: $110–141
Special activities: Pack
trips, fly fishing
Airport: Jackson Hole or
Salt Lake City
Guest capacity: 20

Moose, coyotes, and other wildlife are commonly sighted in the Gros Ventre region where the Darwin Ranch is located. (Both photos by Scott McKinley)

Each day dudes grab their saddlebags packed with a lunch and head off on a new adventure. (Photo by Elizabeth Clair Flood)

Notes from a Dream World

Excerpts from the diary of Jana Fisher

December 10th

This morning was really marvelous. We woke up to a big snow storm. Eggs Benedict and Vivaldi for breakfast. Some drawing. Loring doing carpentry. Tea break. I should add that by the time we eat and sit around or Loring plays the piano the morning is half gone. Most wonderful feeling of no rush. I really get into this style. . . . A coyote barking way below in the valley. What a life. Soon I will have been here four weeks. Somehow it seems more like home than anyplace I remember since being a kid. . . .

December 16th

What I've learned to do: roll cigarettes, split wood, play chess. Last night amazing duck dinner for two. . . .

December 22nd

Yesterday's blizzard produced a new world. No tracks. Big drifts, snow cornices on the buildings. We have a game of trying to stay on the old trails buried beneath the new snow. If you don't you go in up to the knees.

Opened a bale of hay for Oedipus. It had little pressed purple and yellow flowers. Spring.

Watched a moose slide down a hill.

Made sugar cookies. . . .

January 10th

. . . Oedipus biting the cats and licking the picture window of the playroom. Well, they're coming to get us and take us away.

summer. "I never liked crowds," Loring said.

The ranch is gloriously isolated. Red hills loom; horses graze in green pastures that stretch for miles. Other than a few ranch vehicles, there are no automobiles. The main activities are riding, fishing, eating, spotting wildlife, and sleeping. On special evenings, Loring sits at his piano, filling the rustic main lodge with the sounds of Bach or Beethoven.

Guests, who enjoy the ranch in the summer and winter, choose the Darwin because they want a simple and rustic setting. No one cares who you are or what you do. A guest earns respect by telling a good story or cooking a trout almandine picnic in the wilderness.

Said one Darwin dude, "If the brochure said, 'Howdy, enjoy our gift shop, square dance, kiddie activities, outdoor BBQs,' we threw it out."

In the midst of the Gros Ventre Wilderness, the Darwin is one of the most isolated dude ranches. (Photo by Elizabeth Clair Flood)

After a morning ride and several hours of fishing, a guest cooks up trout almandine on the banks of the Gros Ventre River. (Photo by Elizabeth Clair Flood)

What could be more adventuresome than building your own igloo in the isolated wilderness of the Gros Ventre? (Photo courtesy Loring Woodman)

Eatons' Ranch

WOLF, WYOMING 82844

"**G**rub pile, come and get it or we'll throw it away," bellowed Uncle Howard across a frost-covered camp. From two large tents, sleepy-eyed and saddle sore, men and women groped toward the meat tent where waiters served hot mush, pancakes, eggs and bacon. At 8:30 A.M., a menagerie of lawyers, debutantes, and well-to-do—110 of them—climbed on their horses and hit the trail. In their absence, maids made up the tepees. It was 1916 in Glacier National Park. The park had only been open six years to travelers on horseback or on foot.

Howard Eaton, the first dude rancher, knew Glacier and Yellowstone parks better than anyone at the time. He knew the passes and the passwords and loved to show eastern tenderfeet the country's magnificent secrets. This gentleman host's knack for guiding dudes through the wilderness would have a profound effect on the future of dude ranching for years to come.

The Eaton brothers—Howard, Willis, and Alden—started ranching in 1879 in Medora, North Dakota. Eastern friends aching for a western adventure traveled to see the brothers soon after. They stacked themselves on the floor or crowded five and six to a bed like sardines, and ate ranch grub. They wanted to be cowboys and hunt wild game.

After serving 2,200 free meals one year and having only one guest offer to pay for their courtesy, the Eatons decided to charge their guests for room, board, and a saddle horse. Thus the first *dudes* were born. This family was said to have been the first to use the term to mean a paying guest from the East.

In 1903 the brothers sold their Custer Trail Ranch and moved to Wolf, Wyoming. The Eatons asked their dudes not to join them the first summer, but to no avail: seventy showed up in Wolf, demanding to help build up the ranch. And they wanted to pay. "They slept in tents, on the ground, ate off ironing boards, or anything else that would hold a plate, filled lamps, cleaned the new cabins as soon as the

Right: Woolly chaps were the height of fashion at Eatons' Ranch, circa 1918. (Photo courtesy Norina Shields.)

Facing Page: Dude girls kick back at the stables, the hub of the ranch, circa 1950. (Photo courtesy Eatons' Ranch)

Eatons' Ranch

(307) 655–9285
Season: June 1–October 1
Rates weekly: adults $925, 17 and
   under $725, plus 6% sales tax and 15%
   gratuity
Special activities: Overnight horseback
   riding, fly fishing, swimming
Airport: Sheridan
Guest capacity: 125

builders moved out so they could move in, helped with beds and dishes—and paid for the privilege."

Eatons' Ranch, a 7,000-acre spread at the base of the Big Horn Mountains, accommodating 125 guests and a cavvy of 200 horses, is the granddaddy of dude ranches.

It does have electricity instead of kerosene now. There are baths in most cabins instead of men, and women's bath-houses; there's a pop machine; women now wear Levi's instead of fringed riding skirts; no one plays a lawn game called mumblety-peg anymore; and an old stage-coach pulled by a team of four horses no longer picks up dudes and their trunks at the Ranchester train station. Other than that, little has changed since the ranch's beginnings. The Eaton family still provides an authentic dude-ranch vacation for the modern-day dude.

Above: Eaton dudes often mingled with Indian tribes during their pack trips throughout Wyoming and Montana. (Photo courtesy Norina Shields)

Top left: Helping harvest the hay was just one of the many chores dudes enjoyed on the ranch, circa 1912. (Photo courtesy Eatons' Ranch)

Top right: Dudes gather at the stables for a ride, circa 1919. (Photo courtesy Norina Shields)

Vacation Prices, Mid-1930s

July and August:
$55 per week for each grownup.
$50 per week for young people from 13 to 17 years.
$45 per week for children 12 years and under.
Private baths, private living rooms, cottages not occupied to capacity, and single rooms for short visits, are more.
May and June, September and October:
$45 per week for each grownup.
$40 per week for young people from 13 to 17 years.
$35 per week for children 12 years and under.
There is a general reduction of $5 per week for each person who remains an unbroken period of 2 months or longer.
—*"From Eatons' guest brochure"*

Left: This pony obviously enjoys being groomed by his little caretaker. (Photo courtesy Eatons' Ranch)

Elkhorn Ranch

(SOUTH) SASABE STAR ROUTE 97
TUCSON, ARIZONA 85736
(NORTH) 33133 GALLATIN ROAD,
GALLATIN GATEWAY, MONTANA 59730

Love at first bite.(Photo courtesy Elkhorn Ranch)

Elkhorn isn't just a dude ranch—it's two dude ranches: one in Montana's Gallatin valley and one in Arizona, which extends the Elkhorn's season through the winter. Grace and Ernie Miller's Elkhorn, established south of Bozeman in 1922, is the only ranch left that exists both in the north and the south and is still managed by the same family, despite ownership of the northern ranch by former guests.

Shortly after the Millers were married in 1922, they made a deposit of $250 on the ranch in Montana and the place was theirs. They had four dudes that first summer; the guests piled in a cabin and the Millers slept under a tree. Today the ranch is managed by Linda Miller, Grace and Ernie's granddaughter. Elkhorn south was established in 1945 and is now run by Charley Miller, one of their grandsons.

Christmas is the busiest time at Elkhorn in Tucson. Although Santa Claus looks a bit out of place among saguaro cacti and cowboys singing around the bonfire, he has been visiting the Elkhorn for years. In preparation for the holiday, dudes ride into the forest and pick out a piñon pine for the main lodge. Guests and crew are then responsible for decorating the boughs. On Christmas Eve, Charley Miller squats under the tree and passes out presents to a corral full of guests. On Christmas Day the ranch hosts a big dinner, and the crew sings Christmas carols and a few western ditties; it's strictly a buckaroo chorus.

In Montana, guests sleep inside rustic log cabins warmed by woodstoves and Hudson Bay blankets. In the south, the cabins are adobe. At both ranches, riding is the main activity. While northern dudes enjoy climbing steep mountains and galloping through high mountain meadows, southern dudes sally up rocky trails past prickly pear and ocotillo to some of the most exquisite posts for viewing truly wide-open spaces and for stargazing in the evenings. While northern dudes are likely to see bear, moose, and deer, southern dudes cross paths with javelina, mountain lion, and a variety of birds.

"A lot of husbands come because their wives drag them out West. Because the wife went on a golf trip, the husband has agreed to do what she wants. When people get out here, though, something happens. One New York career woman called it her "Elkhorn fix," Jan Miller says. "Another man is now hooked on watching westerns and roping the chairs in his living room."

"I didn't know cowboys rode mules!"
(Photo courtesy Elkhorn Ranch)

Some seasoned dudes chew the fat at the corral.
(Photo courtesy Elkhorn Ranch)

Christmas Greetings from Elkhorn

Winter's heavy blanket covers everything at Elkhorn except the trail to the wood pile and the mailbox, and the spirit of the ranch which our many friends have helped to create."

"You will all be with us in thought as we gather here on Christmas and feast on wild meat and drink a toast to your health, wealth and happiness."

"The children and crew join us in wishing you a MERRY CHRISTMAS and sending sincere hopes for the coming year."

—*Elkhorn Ranch December 25, 1944*
(A piece of sagebrush was tucked into every greeting.)

Ernie Miller serves up a hearty breakfast for a hungry dude. (Photo courtesy Elkhorn Ranch)

Elkhorn South:

(602) 822-1040
Season: Mid-November–April
Rates weekly: $840, special rates for children
Special activities: Swimming, tennis
Airport: Tucson
Guest capacity: 32

Elkhorn North:

(406) 995–4291
Season: Mid-April–mid-September
Rates weekly: adults $1,075, children $975
Special activities: Fly-fishing
Airport: Bozeman or West Yellowstone
Guest capacity: 55

Every Saturday in the 1940s and 1950s, dudes gathered to listen to the Texaco broadcast from the Metropolitan Opera. Often the burro Bridget wandered up from the barn and brayed along with the soprano aria. (Photo courtesy Elkhorn Ranch)

G Bar M

P.O. BOX AE
CLYDE PARK, MONTANA 59018

Being able to ride in the high country, smelling the pine and the sage, seeing the changing colors of sunlight and clouds on the sage-covered hills, watching the sun go down over the snow-capped mountains and owning a beautiful horse was my way of life. . . . To me, ranching isn't just a way of life; it is my reason for living," wrote Mary Leffingwell in her book, *Diamonds in the Snow.*

In 1898, Mary's father, then twenty-three, hopped a train in Zanesville, Ohio, for Big Timber, Montana, with a homemade bedroll and all he possessed in a round-top trunk. Arriving in Big Timber, this young man went to the Grand Hotel in search of a job, as he was told that was where the big sheepmen and cattlemen gathered when they came to town. He landed a job on a ranch west of town. A few years later, he had enough money to homestead a property in the Clyde Park area; thirty years later, this ranch grew to twenty square miles. When in 1942 the family sold some of the original Bridgman Stock Ranch, the G Bar M was established on what was left.

Encouraged by the Northern Pacific Railroad dude-ranch campaign and the pinch of the depression, in 1934 the family started taking in guests to supplement their income. At first the Leffingwells were reluctant to jump into the guest business, but they soon learned to love sharing their country with guests.

"I feel our way of life has started to disappear and is going faster with each generation," says George Leffingwell, Mary's son. "Here we like to help people learn what the West is all about and what it used to be about." Mary says when guests chat with George and his wife Patricia Pisciotta, they get "an education without realizing

Dudes arrive for a ranch vacation toting suitcases full of cowboy clothing, circa 1930. (Photo courtesy G Bar M)

After a long ride, dudes gather on the ridge for a peek at the view. Patricia Leffingwell says some dudes make drastic changes in their lives, such as quitting their nine-to-five jobs and moving west after a stay at the G Bar M. (Photo courtesy G Bar M)

Food always tastes better outside.
(Photo courtesy G Bar M)

George Leffingwell and dudes fixing fence. (Photo by Betty Engle LeVin, courtesy of the G Bar M)

it." Guests on this ranch get a taste of real ranching life. Whatever needs doing becomes the activity for the day, whether it's mending fence or tending the cattle.

At the end of the day, guests sit down with the family for a homemade dinner and conversation. Discussion topics swing from the day's ride to the condition of the cattle to current events to the guests' interests. "We learn as much from our guests as they learn from us," says George.

"When new guests arrive, they sometimes can't tell whether people are guests, help or family. Everyone is treated the same," says Mary.

According to Patricia, "Guests relax over the week, get off the fast track and begin to appreciate the simpler values in life. They get back in touch with nature."

A young dude is thrilled to find breakfast. (Photo by Betty Engle LeVin, courtesy of the G Bar M)

Favorite G Bar M Ranch Recipes

BARLEY STEW

This is a versatile recipe that can be used with either raw or cooked meat—beef, venison or lamb.

In a heavy kettle or Dutch oven, melt 2 tablespoons margarine or bacon grease.

Brown:
2 pounds cubed stew meat with
1 1/2 cups pearl barley
If using cooked meat, add to browned barley.

Add:
3 cups beef stock or
2 tablespoons beef soup base dissolved in 3 cups boiling water
1 tablespoon Worcestershire sauce
1 teaspoon salt
1/4 teaspoon garlic salt
Dash of Tabasco sauce
1 large can (2 1/2 cups) tomatoes
4 stalks celery, chopped

Mix and cover. Bake 325° for 2 hours. (May need more liquid.)

BROWNIE PUDDING

Serves 6
A favorite of chocolate lovers.

Mix in greased baking dish:
1/2 cup flour
1/2 cup sugar
1 teaspoon baking powder
1/2 teaspoon salt
1 tablespoon cocoa
1/4 cup milk
1 tablespoon melted shortening
1 teaspoon vanilla

Mix into a stiff dough. Spread level.

Sprinkle with 1/4 cup brown sugar.

Dissolve 1 tablespoon cocoa in 1 cup boiling water. Pour on top. Don't mix.

Bake at 350° for 30 to 40 minutes.

Serve with whipped cream or ice cream.

Parents love to take children to a dude ranch because they can turn their youngsters loose and be assured they'll find something to do. (Photo by Betty Engle LeVin, courtesy G Bar M)

G Bar M Ranch:

(406) 686–4423
Season: May 15–September 15
Rates weekly:
$640–730 adults,
$550–590 children
Special activities:
Fly fishing
Airport: Bozeman
Guest capacity: 15

HF Bar

SADDLESTRING, WYOMING 82840

Dean Thomas's illustrations and Christmas cards were avidly collected by the dudes. Besides being a fine artist, he worked for the HF Bar for over fifty years as a good cowhand, dude wrangler, plumber, and secretary-treasurer. (Card courtesy of Margi Schroth)

A young dude girl in a black cowboy hat and an oilskin coat steps off her pony and hands the reins to a wrangler. He teases her. She laughs. Dangling her arms over the corral fence, she tosses her ponytail, shoots back a sly remark, and waits.

"My favorite thing is to hang out at the corral," says twenty-year-old Whitney, who has been spending summers at the HF Bar for many years. "I get in from my ride at 11 A.M. and I stay at the corral until noon harassing the wranglers." After the evening ride she does the same.

Whitney remembers as a child jumping rope and playing Four Square in the corral, going on hayrides, and leading the kiddie dinner rides. As a young woman, she loves galloping across the hills and meadows and chumming at Salt Creek—a hangout under the stars.

The ranch was started in 1902 by Frank "Skipper" Horton, who in the late 1800s was diagnosed as being color-blind. This was devastating news for an Iowa-born, aspiring surgeon. He was told that living in the country might cure him, so he headed out to Wyoming, where he eventually established a successful cattle ranch on the 10,000-acre property called Saddlestring, Wyoming. However, about 1915 he turned the place into a dude ranch because too many of his friends were demanding to spend summers there. They even agreed to design their own cabins, which were dreamed up in the late evenings and drawn on the backs of napkins. Today these funky buildings hidden in the trees still accommodate guests. The cabin named "The House that Jack Built" is so convoluted it resembles a tree house—and kids adore it.

Until just recently the ranch was run by two women, Henriette "Hank" Horton and Margi Schroth. Today Margi and daughters Lily and Cara ride herd over the HF

HF Bar Ranch:

(307) 684–2487
Season: June 1–
    September 15
Rates daily: $130
    adults, discounts for
    children
Special activities: Pack
    trips, swimming,
    sporting clay shooting
Airport: Sheridan
Guest capacity: 95

A wrangler checks on the herd before dudes arrive at the barn for a morning ride. (Photo by Elizabeth Clair Flood)

Bar. Other than updating the water and sewer systems, building a swimming pool, and adding big, splashy bath towels to the cabins, the HF Bar hasn't changed since its beginning.

Although the dude-ranching heyday was in the 1920s, Margi believes ranches are reliving that time—glamour and all. Dudes like young Whitney find the HF Bar setting romantic. "I think a dude ranch is a place where you embrace that solitary, almost mystical, life of the cowboy. He is part of the American legend. You come out to experience that, to listen to that silence and the lonesome howl of the coyote. There are very few places left in this entire world where you can experience silence and simplicity."

Frank O. Horton and cowboys camp out during cattle work in the 1930s. In the 1970s, when the HF Bar decided to focus more on their dudes, they pulled out of the cattle business. Today they call themselves a working ranch. They harvest their own hay, care for their horse herd, and pasture a small herd of cattle in the winter. (Photo courtesy King's Saddlery)

Far right: After a morning's activities, dudes looked forward to enjoying a delicious meal served outdoors. An early brochure promised guests they would relax so much at the HF Bar, that when they returned home, "Years will have dropped from your shoulders like feathers from a molting hen. And you will come back again." (Photo courtesy Margi Schroth)

The HF Bar barn was built in 1911. Today it is the center of the ranch. (Photo courtesy King's Saddlery)

Hunewill Ranch

P.O. Box 368 Bridgeport, California 93517 (Summer)
P.O. Box 205 Wellington NV 89444 (Winter)

People of all ages enjoy "duding it up" for a week or two. (Photo courtesy Hunewill Ranch)

Facing page: Lenore and Stanley Hunewill show off a string of trout, circa 1936. (Photo courtesy Hunewill Ranch)

A businessman from California wanted to chase dogies and ride like a Texas cowpuncher into the sunset—kind of like Billy Crystal in *City Slickers*. After riding sixty miles in the Hunewill Ranch cattle drive, however, he discovered his western experience far exceeded his romantic expectations. What he didn't bank on were the new friends he'd make and the power of the scenery.

"If you ride all day on a horse with others, you develop quite intimate relationships," he says. "And the scenery is so spectacular—the kind that restores the soul."

The Hunewill Ranch was started by N. B. Hunewill, originally from Maine. In 1861 he built a sawmill on Eagle Creek and later began cattle ranching in Buckeye and the Bridgeport Valley. Since 1930 the Hunewills have been hosting dudes.

Every fall, the Hunewills invite dudes to help them drive 400–700 head of cattle from their summer ranch in Bridgeport, California, sixty miles to their ranch in Nevada. Although there may be occasion to sleep out by the chuck wagon, most return to the ranch and a hot shower every evening. The dudes shuttle back to the cattle in the morning. Every day the drive covers approximately fifteen miles. A hearty lunch is served out of the chuck wagon each day.

"Eighty percent of the drive you are walking along shouting," the businessman dude says. "The other twenty percent of the time you are chasing the cattle out of the bushes or looking for them."

For the Hunewills, the cattle drive is a time to enjoy family and tradition. "As a kid, being on the cattle drive wasn't like I was really working. It was mostly a lot of fun. No worries," says Betsy Hunewill Elliott, great-great-granddaughter of the ranch's founder. "There is a sense of helping out—community—like an Amish barn raising. A cattle drive is really a neat way to bring people together. I love the joking and bantering—

Hunewill Ranch:

(619) 932–7710
Season: Mid-May–end
September
Rates weekly: $750–900
Special activities: Cattle
drive in November
Airport: Reno, NV and
Bridgeport, CA
Guest capacity: 45
Special children's
program

and the country."

The family thinks the Hunewill Ranch is the perfect place to work. And hundreds of guests agree it's the perfect place to be a cowboy or cowgirl for a week. After ten years on the cattle drive, the California businessman still enjoys the peace and camaraderie he finds there.

Every year, the folks on the drive stop on a knoll where a former member of the cattle drive had her ashes scattered. And for a little time the group is silent. At this moment the dudes know there is more to a cattle drive than playing cowboy in the sage.

Above: Dudes blow off steam on the volleyball court. (Photo by William H. Logan, courtesy Hunewill Ranch)

Top Right: Guests help move the mamas and calves to new pasture. (Photo by William A. Logan, courtesy Hunewill Ranch)

Below: The scenery at Hunewill is breathtaking in all seasons. (Photo by William A. Logan, courtesy Hunewill Ranch)

Hunewill Circle H Ranch Recipe

DELICIOUS COOKIES
1 cup margarine
1 cup brown sugar
1 cup white sugar
1 cup oil
1 egg
1 tsp. vanilla
1 tsp. cream of tartar
3 1/2 cups flour
1 cup quick oatmeal
1 cup coconut
1 cup crispy rice cereal
1 cup chopped nuts
    Blend margarine, sugars, oil, and eggs. Add cream of tartar and flour. Add rest of ingredients. Drop by spoonfuls onto a greased cookie sheet. Press flat with a fork. Bake at 350° for 12 minutes. Makes approximately 100.

Above: Ever since *City Slickers*, cattle drives have attracted more dudes than ever before. (Photo courtesy Frederick S. Wyle) Right: LeNore Hunewill (center) stands with two guests about to hit the trail. (Photo courtesy Hunewill Ranch)

Klick's K Bar L Ranch

P.O. BOX 287
AUGUSTA, MONTANA 59410

Sweaty horse blankets hang out to dry in front of the head wrangler's cabin. (Photo by Elizabeth Clair Flood)

Surprisingly, the best access to Klick's K Bar L Ranch is over water. Guests are picked up in Great Falls and driven to Gibson Lake, where they board a speedboat. As they near the ranch, a surrey pulled by two mules, Tic and Tac, is at their service to take them the rest of the way. Once a dude crosses the bridge into the ranch, the rest of the world disappears.

In parts of Montana, dude ranching started at the train depot.

"When the railroad came to Augusta, Montana, people started showing up wanting to go into the mountains. So everybody just started hanging around the depot, waiting to find somebody who would grubstake them. It was pioneering, brand-new," says Dick Klick, a third-generation dude rancher.

"Once my Uncle Sam went to town to get some groceries. When he swung by the depot, there was this guy with a woman, and they wanted to go back into the hills and spend the winter. And, boy, this guy had money! So they all got in the wagon and went downtown, and this fellow bought hams and loads of supplies. Sam really thought he had something and headed home. At about the time Sam and this gentleman were headed off to Shelby, Montana, to watch the great Jack Dempsey/Tommy Gibbons fight, the lady got tired of it in the mountains and went to town. Well, quickly the FBI picked her up. The gentleman was a bank embezzler. So the agents got Sam's meal ticket, and he didn't get to go to the fight. This is just an example of how the old-timers were doing dude business."

More often than not, though, these depot dudes worked out just fine.

"For many years our ranch was a closely guarded secret. Our guests wouldn't tell anybody. They wouldn't pass on where they went in the summer because they

Klick's K Bar L Ranch

(406) 467–2771 (summer),
(406) 562–3589 (winter)
Season: May 1–December 1
Rates: On request
Special activities: Pack trips, fly-fishing, swimming
Airport: Great Falls
Guest capacity: 30

The Klick family was trained in the outfitting business before they took in dudes for the summer. Today the ranch still hosts hunters. (Photo courtesy Klick's K Bar L)

The Guests' Favorite Recipe

SWISS ONIONS

4 cups Walla Walla sweet onions, sliced
about 4 or 5)
2 Tbsp. butter
1/2 can cream of chicken soup
1/2 cup milk
1 tsp. Worcestershire sauce
3/4 cup grated Swiss cheese
4 slices French bread
Butter
Parmesan cheese
Paprika

Sauté onions in the butter, stirring until limp and tender. Place in a buttered 8"x8" baking dish. Combine the soup, milk, and Worcestershire sauce. Pour over the onions. Top with grated Swiss cheese.

Press the bread slices on top of the onion-cheese mixture. Lightly butter the top of each slice. Sprinkle with Parmesan cheese and paprika to taste. Bake in a 350° oven for about 25 minutes, or until bread begins to brown.
Serves 4.

Deciding on the perfect fly. (Photo by Brown, courtesy Klick's K Bar L)

didn't want any more people out here. That was all fine until they started crossing over the Great Divide," said Dick Klick, owner. Then the Klicks started doing a little more advertising.

"The K Bar L was built as a dude ranch, no question about that," Dick says. He is very satisfied with the lifestyle. And his wife, Nancy, adds, "It isn't every industry that you can have all these great friends and get paid to visit with them." K Bar L is one of the oldest dude-ranch outfitters in Montana. The ranch has always been known for its pack trips, fishing, fall hunting, and miles of breathtaking riding country.

Tucked up against one-and-a-half million acres of wilderness area, including the Great Bear, the Scapegoat, and the largest of all three—the Bob Marshall—the ranch is exquisite and remote. As the sign on the gate reads: "KLICK'S K BAR L, BEYOND ALL ROADS."

Right: The Klick's K Bar L backyard encompasses approximately a million-and-a-half acres of wilderness. (Photo courtesy Klick's K Bar L)

Below: Dudes find the main lodge, built in 1927, a comfortable place to linger just about anytime of the day. (Photo courtesy Klick's K Bar L)

Above: Emil Klick rests his pack string: Cookie, Beans, Prunes, and Primo. (Photo courtesy Klick's K Bar L)

Lazy K Bar Ranch

P. O. Box 550
Big Timber, Montana 59011

The ranch really hasn't changed much in the last 73 years. And the guests don't want it changed," Tack Van Cleve says. "Of course, we have added things like a coin-operated washer and dryer for the guests' convenience. We added a swimming pool in 1940 and, well, that's really about it. The cabins, of course, have to be well maintained. You have to replace logs—the bottom ones—every thirty years or so. We've also added bathrooms and electric water heaters to all the cabins."

Paul "Tack" Van Cleve runs the family ranch, which has been operating since 1880, with his sisters Barbara and Carol. Lazy K Bar is a 22,000-acre spread under the Crazy Mountains in Big Timber, Montana, where four generations of Van Cleves have grown up and passed along the tradition of western hospitality.

In 1880, Paul Van Cleve, originally from Minnesota, moved west, purchased property, and started ranching on Porcupine Butte. Some of the area characters he knew included Calamity Jane, "Liver Eating" Johnston, and Plenty Coups, chief of the Crow.

"You see, my great-grandparents always had a full house of guests from back East and abroad. They had a thirty-six-room ranch house, so they had lots of room for guests. And they were nonpaying guests. My grandparents decided that if they were going to be entertaining easterners all summer long, every summer, they should do as Teddy Roosevelt and the Eaton brothers did—start charging them and providing them with their own living quarters—and it sort of evolved."

With the help of a Norwegian broadaxe man, the family built cabins and filled them with hand-built rustic furniture and antiques from the original ranch house.

In all of Tack's fifty-eight years, he's never spent a summer away from the family

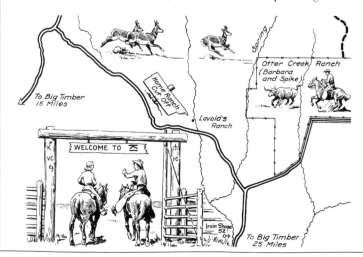

Lazy K Bar Ranch

(406) 537–4404
Season: June 23–Labor Day
Rates weekly: $600–940 per person
Special activities: Overight rides, swimming, fossil beds, working cattle
Airport: Billings or Bozeman
Guest capacity: 45

ranch. "It was just instilled in us that the ranch came before everything else," Tack says. "And I don't think anybody drummed it into us. We just always felt that our own personal plans came second to the ranch. As young as six years old, I was helping butcher and pluck chickens and make the ice cream. We had to sit and crank this ice-cream maker; we were allowed to lick the paddles for an hour of work, and we thought it was a swell trade-off."

In addition to riding, guests at Lazy K Bar like to fish, hike in the mountains, swim, and generally relax.

And anyone who visits the ranch today will be following in the tradition of clientele like the Duponts, Rockefellers, Fords, and a slew of Princetonions, who, over the years, rollicked at the ranch, enjoying the honest-to-goodness western experience that is at the center of the Lazy K Bar's reputation.

A Glimpse from the Past

Spike Van Cleve wrote a book about dude ranching and recalled some of his favorite experiences. Following is one:

"I was changing a latigo when I heard one of the wranglers sort of choke. I looked up and there the two girls were, peering through the corral gate and grinning from ear to ear. I stepped around the old pony in front of me to say good morning, got a clear look at them and saw why the wrangler'd choked. I did, too!

They were sure outfitted! I may be a little vague about their top halves, but it seems to me they had on black hats with tie-downs, bandanas and gaudy shirts. The rest, I remember a lot better. Boots, spurs, and tight, narrow batwing chaps. But I guess nobody'd told them you wore britches with leggings, for all they had under them were their drawers, pretty pink ones!"

—From *40 Years' Gatherin's* by Spike Van Cleve

Founders, owners and proprietors of Lazy K Bar Ranch, Helen and Paul Van Cleve, Jr. (Photo courtesy Lazy K Bar Ranch)

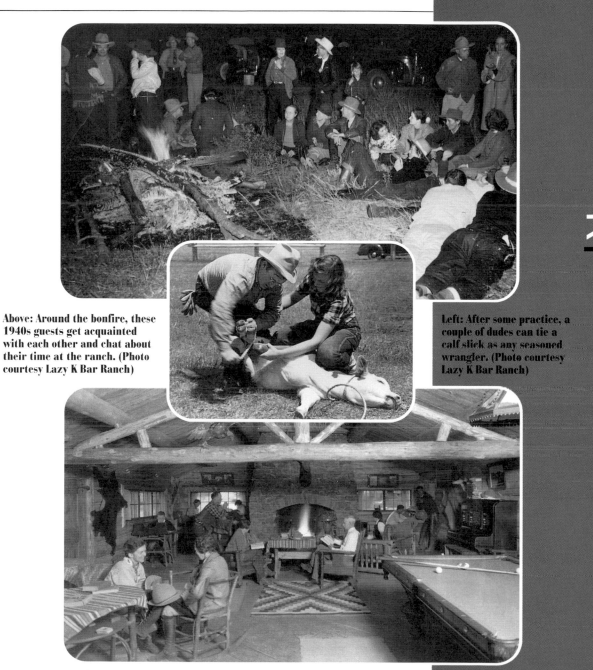

Above: Around the bonfire, these 1940s guests get acquainted with each other and chat about their time at the ranch. (Photo courtesy Lazy K Bar Ranch)

Left: After some practice, a couple of dudes can tie a calf slick as any seasoned wrangler. (Photo courtesy Lazy K Bar Ranch)

Visiting and relaxing inside the lodge is a favorite pastime. The facilities accommodate a wide variety of interests. (Photo courtesy Lazy K Bar Ranch)

Moose Head Ranch

P.O. Box 214
Moose, Wyoming 83012

On May 26, 1927, Eva Grace Sanford homesteaded property on Spread Creek, about thirty-three miles south of Yellowstone and directly across the valley from the majestic Teton mountain range. Soon after, she married Fred Topping and started a dude ranch in an area called Elk, later to be named Moose.

Eva always had plenty to do. As Betsy Bernfeld reported from her extensive research on the Moose Head Ranch, "Eva Topping was a homesteader, ranch wife, business woman, school teacher, post-mistress and historian—filling by herself almost every conceivable role played by women in pioneer days."

The Toppings' place was a cozy retreat for dudes in the summer and for hunters in the fall. Guests, who paid $14 a day for accommodations, food, and entertainment, were packed in cabins and ate in a dining room so jammed that waitresses could barely get around the chairs to serve.

Since Moose Head Ranch was an operating ranch with cattle, horses, hay, and poultry as its main products, it was nearly self-sufficient. Dudes were treated to fresh beef, poultry, eggs, milk, cream, butter and green vegetables.

In 1967, John and Eleo Mettler, seasoned Jackson Hole dudes and cattle ranchers from the East, purchased the Moose Head from the Toppings. The Mettlers had dreamed of owning a ranch in Jackson where they could take their family for the summer. While they weren't exactly in the market to be dude ranchers, the lifestyle suited them and they soon learned to love and welcome an extended family of dudes.

The ranch, actually inside Grand Teton National Park, is an exquisite retreat where guests live in snug cabins scattered among

Fred entertains a dudette. Today the Moose Head still hosts Sunday sing-alongs where dudes enjoy singing "Home on the Range." (Photo courtesy Teton County Historical Society)

CM Ranch:

(307) 733–3141 (summer),
(904) 877–1431 (winter)
Season: Mid-June–end of August
Rates daily: adults $175, children 6 and under $100
Special activities: Fly fishing
Airport: Jackson Hole
Guest capacity: 40

Arriving out West was an exotic adventure for easterners. This photo, a promotional piece, is probably a staged shot. (Photo courtesy Teton County Historical Society)

Eva Topping cooks up a mean bear stew. (Photo by Herb Pownell, courtesy Teton County Historical Society)

aspen, cottonwood, pines, and small streams. Since the sixties, the Mettlers have replaced the older cabins with modern ones and added a spacious new lodge. The ranch no longer has cattle or chickens; the post office and school are closed; and the moose population is smaller than in the early days—but the atmosphere is still western.

In recent years, the Mettler ranching tradition has been continued by John and Eleo's daughter and son-in-law, Louise and Kit Davenport, who, along with head wrangler Dave Edmiston, make sure each guest receives a vacation perfectly tailored

to his or her needs. Louise spends time with each family, discussing interesting day trips into Yellowstone and suggesting where the best powder rooms and picnic spots are in the park, where to spot wildlife, where anglers will find the biggest fish, and where to see some of the finest western art in Jackson Hole. The Davenports also take care of the day-to-day ranch details and problems, from suggesting white-water trips to arranging babysitting to organizing a Ping-Pong game to help keep everyone entertained.

During the day the only scheduled events are meals and rides. Meals are prepared by a gourmet chef, and riding groups are small. Fly-fishers can enjoy the stocked trout ponds where fishing is done on a catch-and-release basis. Water enthusiasts can take scenic or whitewater float trips down the Snake River. In the evenings guests still gather in the living room or by a campfire to sing or recount the day's events with newfound friends.

When guests pack to leave, they take with them the memory of the exquisite Grand Teton country and of the Moose Head hospitality.

Looking for the Perfect Vacation

April 24th, 1940

Mr. Fred J. Topping
Moose Head Ranch
Elk Post Office
Jackson Hole, Wyoming

Dear Sir:

Another chap (insurance broker) and myself (sportswriter for the *New York Daily News*), being close pals, have decided on a vacation together at a ranch. We're writing to you for advice and particulars.

We don't want anything fancy and if that is what you're offering, please tell us so and we'll drop the matter. We're young (24 and 26) but city-softened and in need of harding up. We want to ride and play rough; swim, but not in a pretty tile pool; eat, but not any French chef concoctions. We'll take steak, rare. We'd much prefer a pack trip, with a couple of nights in the open to fishing. We're not ardent anglers. . . .

We're a bit worried about the weather, however. We don't want to freeze and certainly plan on some sunshine. We mention this because of certain stories from friends who say the snow isn't out in June.

All told we have approximately 27 days. Can you help us?

Above: Fred and Eva chat with guests after dinner. (Photo courtesy Teton County Historical Society)

Inset: A picture postcard of the ranch.

Left: "We lost a milk cow— temporarily at least; the men passed by a cabin, heard a noise, and sure enough, the cow was in the cabin! Had nosed around and unlatched the door, gone inside, and the door swung shut, and there she was, comfortable, except thirsty and hungry—but that isn't the worst—she had climbed on the bed, in an effort to find a way out—and the mess is one for the record. Thank heavens dude season is a few days away." Eva G. Topping, April 30, 1960. (Photo courtesy Teton County Historical Society)

R Lazy S

P.O. BOX 308
TETON VILLAGE, WYOMING 83025

Backed up against Grand Teton National Park and flanking the banks of the Snake River, the R Lazy S Ranch offers the traditional palette of fun and more. Dudes enjoy miles of silent and pristine country. They learn to ride and fly-fish; they see elk, moose, buffalo, deer, ermine, porcupine, birds, bear, and other wildlife. They take whitewater, scenic, and fishing float trips on the Snake River, play golf or tennis down the road, hike in Grand Teton, and visit Yellowstone. Because the R Lazy S is only ten miles from the tourist town of Jackson, other activities include visiting Jackson's fine art galleries, two-stepping at the Million Dollar Cowboy Bar, catching a play at the Pink Garter Theater, or dining out.

The R Lazy S has been providing a family experience in the out-of-doors since 1948, when Robert and Florrelle McConaughy started the guest business. Now owned by Cara and Howard Stirn and managed by Bob and Claire McConaughy, the R Lazy S provides experiences for dudes that many westerners take for granted. For instance, Claire remembers a man from New York City who stepped outside the lodge his first evening at the ranch and called for his family. Claire thought he must have seen a bear. Everyone rushed outside to see the man gazing amazed at the starry sky and beckoning his kids to his side. "Children, that is what stars look like."

Guests and employees remember the early R Lazy S—noted author Owen Wister's original homestead—as a very rustic place. "All I remember from the old ranch was a battle over the good cabins," says former guest and present owner Howard Stirn. "The one my wife and I wanted didn't have a porch or closet. There were wooden pegs to hang your clothes from. It did have a small bathroom, but if Cara wanted to come in, I stood in the bathtub."

"It is such a good feeling to have a place to go where so little has changed," says

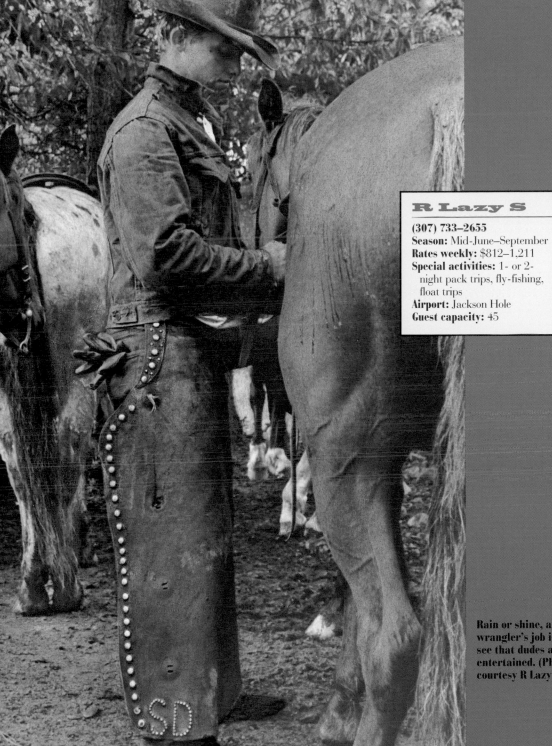

R Lazy S

(307) 733–2655
Season: Mid-June–September
Rates weekly: $812–1,211
Special activities: 1- or 2-
 night pack trips, fly-fishing,
 float trips
Airport: Jackson Hole
Guest capacity: 45

Rain or shine, a
wrangler's job is to
see that dudes are
entertained. (Photo
courtesy R Lazy S)

Cara, who can count on seeing the same flowers, same creatures, same old cabins, and riding the same trails she loved as a child while staying at the Bear Paw Ranch with her parents in the early 1940s.

It only takes one week with the McConaughys and Stirns at the R Lazy S to become bewitched by dude-ranch living and Jackson Hole country. The experience is the kind that makes people cry at the end of the week. Girls kiss their horses goodbye, and families pack bunches of sage-brush into their suitcases. As one eastern man remarked, "It was easier to make friends in one week at the ranch than it has been to make friends in four years at our home."

From the R Lazy S Kitchen

MOOSE BEANS

1 15-oz. can green lima beans
1 15-oz. can butter beans
1 15-oz. can kidney beans
1 16-oz. can B & M baked beans
1/2 lb. bacon, diced
1 medium onion, chopped
1/2 tsp. dry mustard
3/4 cup brown sugar
1/3 cup cider vinegar

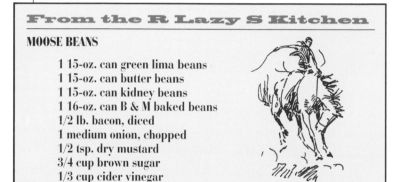

Fry bacon. Remove bacon and sauté onion in drippings. Combine mustard, brown sugar and vinegar. Bring to a boil and add bacon, onion and drippings. Mix with beans. Place in a covered casserole dish. Bake at 350° for 30 minutes. Remove cover and bake an additional 30 minutes. (Marge Bresnahan)

Most of the ranch cabins were built in the forties, and then moved from Grand Teton National Park to the present ranch site. They have all been refurbished and each cabin has its own character. (Photo by Howard Stirn)

Right: Throughout the week, young girls fall head over heels in love with their dude ponies. When it is time to return home at the end of the week, there are always tears. To make the good-bye easier, Bob cuts girls a bit of their horse's mane to take with them. (Photo by Howard Stirn)

Above: For those whose derrieres ache from long, hard rides, a canoe trip is a perfect break. (Photo by Howard Stirn)

Cooling off at the swimming hole. (Photo by Howard Stirn)

7D

P.O. BOX 100
CODY, WYOMING 82414

Sooner or later a dude becomes intrigued with a pack trip—the ultimate western experience. The promise of new vistas, stories of grizzlies in camp, and the goose-bump thrill of traveling in the wilderness goads a greenhorn to stray from the comforts of the ranch.

Although no one nowadays leads pack trips in the grand style of Howard Eaton—who in the 1880s led tours of Yellowstone with waiters, wranglers, and maids—there are still plenty of first-class trips available for the adventurous or old-fashioned traveler.

At 6 A.M. David Dominick of the 7D Ranch rouses guests from slumber. "Get yourself some coffee, then let's pack up. We need to be on the trail by nine."

"Do you have a warm coat? Riding gloves? A slicker? A pocketknife? Binoculars? A flashlight? A gun?" asked an experienced pack-trip guide just the day before. "Everything but the gun," I said.

Packing light and practical is the point, as all equipment is packed tightly into canvas panniers strapped onto mules or pack horses with a diamond hitch. Extras such as rain gear, lunch, and water slip into one's own saddlebag.

The trip begins just outside the ranch boundaries. The sound of hooves, the clink of spurs, and light snow flurries entice the group forward and up to the final destination—the Hoodoo Mountains on the border of Yellowstone Park. Zigzagging up switchbacks to the boundary line of Shoshone National Forest, behind a string of pack mules blanketed with snowflakes, a dude feels the tingling sensation that early explorers must have felt as they ascended into uncharted territory.

Pack trips have always been an important part of the charm of the 7D Ranch. The tradition has continued unbroken from the 1950s, when David's father, Wyoming general practitioner Dr. Dewey Dominick, with his wife, Lee, purchased the 7D. Pack trips are not for everyone, however. Fewer

Cookie Hanson served up some fine grub at the 7D. The ranch was certainly not a place to start a diet. (Photo courtesy 7D Ranch)

Dude ranchers were the first to define western-style interiors. As in the lodge at the 7D, dude ranches featured rooms with Navajo rugs, handmade furniture, and western and Native American memorabilia decorating the walls. (Photo by Robert Weiglein, © 1993)

7D Ranch:

(307) 587–3997 summer
(307) 587–9885 winter
Season: June 4–September 17
Rates weekly: $1,265
Special activities: Pack trips, fly fishing, hiking
Airport: Yellowstone Regional in Cody
Guest capacity: 30 Special children's program for ages 6–12.

ranches offer pack trips now than in the early days. Pack trips are a challenge to run, and many dudes don't have the luxury time such trips require.

"The greatest experience in the world is to have a string of mules and a bell mare and to head out with a map and go for ten days wherever your instincts lead you," David says. "As you get into the rhythm, the days get easier, and as the dudes get into the rhythm they begin to struggle less against it. They sleep better on the ground and they sit down, cross their legs, and hang onto their dinner plate and eat their food. They begin to slow down a little and relax."

As the sun disappears over snow-capped peaks and campfire smoke seeps into clothing, David begins a story, and a dude can almost hear Doc Dominick's voice echoing from days past: "Take a look around you. Ain't it great?"

Right: David Dominick, one of the 7D's owners, is now in charge of the ranch. Here he serves up a mean barbecue. (Photo by Robert Weiglein, © 1993)

Far right: Loading panniers with the essentials for a pack trip is an art. Upon reaching camp in the high country, no one wants to discover they've left their dry clothes, dinner, or tent back at the ranch. (Photo by Robert Weiglein, © 1993)

Below right: Dude ponies quench their thirst in Sunlight Creek. (Photo by Robert Weiglein, © 1993)

The Priorities From the 7D Ranch Staff Manual

simple statement of what our summer business is all about seems in order:

Priority #1 The care, protection and welfare of the 7D Ranch Horse Herd

Priority #2 The safety of the Dudes and quality of their vacation

Priority #3 The health and enjoyment of the staff

A strange list? Perhaps. But if each of these is tended to in order of priority most of the summer should fall into place.

Horses first.

Recognize that horses are the life-blood of the ranch; they represent our single most significant capital investment; they offer us the best insurance against accidents that money can buy; they also are the most vulnerable and needy creatures on the ranch.

Recognize that horses are individuals: moody, unpredictable, heavy, powerful, dangerous, beautiful, sometimes affectionate, and alternatively exasperating animals.

6 Ranch

P.O. BOX 979
LIVINGSTON, MONTANA 59047

Young Sandra was born a cowgirl and grew up on the 63 Ranch. Her first real kiss was delivered by a ranch guest—western artist and writer Will James. "My mother was horrified," she says. (Photo courtesy 63 Ranch)

In 1931, Virginia, a New York city gal, asked her girlfriend to join her on a dude-ranch vacation in Montana. The two plotted and planned, and when summer came, they took the train from there to Livingston. Upon arrival at the Livingston depot, thoughts of sticky, uncomfortable days on the train were forgotten, and the two looked forward to their stay at the Triangle 7, nestled in the Absaroka Mountains.

At the Fourth of July rodeo in Livingston, Jinnie met Paul Christensen, rancher of the neighboring 63, and after that, she spent much of her time courting love. After the vacation ended, the two corresponded. Paul took forty-five-minute trips to town to call Jinnie in her New York apartment and visited her in New York several times. They were married in 1933, and Jinnie has lived in Montana on the 63 Ranch, an operating cattle and dude ranch, ever since.

Today Jinnie, her daughter Sandra and son-in-law Bud, and their son Jeff run the 63, which, as one of the older dude ranches established in

Montana, is included on the National Register of Historic Places.

The ranch—420 acres on Mission Creek—had been purchased in 1929 by Paul Christensen and his brother and sister. Having worked and lived in the Yellowstone area, the three siblings were familiar with dude ranches and were intrigued enough to try one themselves.

They knew that building the place into a successful venture would be a challenge, but they were determined. As Sandra wrote in her history of the 63 Ranch, "The first three dudes were three young men from Chicago: one quite wealthy, one had less money, and the third was very poor. So we charged the rich one and the second what they could pay and let the poor one come for nothing."

The ranch has changed little since the early days, says Jinnie. "We didn't have bathrooms then." Kerosene lamps were traded in for power in 1948, cabins were added over the years, and there is a phone.

When Paul Christensen passed away, there was no question in Jinnie and

**Dudes flash the latest western fashions in the 1930s.
(Photo courtesy 63 Ranch)**

Sandra's minds that they would continue the family tradition. "I love practically everything about dude ranching," Jinnie says. "It's nice to meet people and entertain them. You don't go into it to make money. You make a living, that's all."

Sitting on the couch by the fireplace, Sandra squeezes her mom's hand. Their family loyalty is obvious, and it's one of the main things that endears the 63 Ranch to the hundreds of dudes who have spent time here.

The Lancaster Family, the 63 Ranch's first guests in 1930, just after arriving. (Photo courtesy 63 Ranch)

Below: There is never a dull moment at the corral. (Photo courtesy 63 Ranch)

Far right: A bedroom set built circa 1930 by Don Hindman, a former craftsman for furniture maker Thomas Molesworth of Cody, Wyoming, and Sandra's uncle, decorates a guest cabin. (Photo courtesy 63 Ranch)

Having worked out West and sampled the dude business in Yellowstone, Rose, Paul, and Jo Christensen were determined to create their own dude outfit. Building the ranch was a struggle, but they never lost sight of their dream. (Photo courtesy 63 Ranch)

Letter from a Guest

Dear Sandra,   August 14

    I had to write before much more time passed to thank you and your family for sharing your beautiful Montana home and for making our vacation the best we've ever had. There were several tearful moments driving home as we reflected on so many special memories. . . .

    We thought you might like to hear some of the memories that are indelibly printed on our minds—(are guests often inspired to share these thoughts with you?)

    The gentle sound of horses hooves as we watched your silhouette, on horseback, against a grayish pink Montana sky at dusk.

    Friends we'd known for less than a week, seemed like years.

    Pogo's tail waving like a flag—leading the way on the trails.

    The extra time you took to explain to Johnny and Kevin special things about horses, saddles, etc.

    Warm, purring kittens in the morning.

    Joe and Gentle Ben's race with John and Homer on that special Saturday when we really let go! (You must have known we needed that.)

    "Star" taking Johnny aside with Sparkle in a crowded corral on the last night just so he could say a special goodbye.

    Kevin's trout swimming in the bathtub.

    Roy—everything you'd expect a cowboy to be and more.

    Chic—friendly from the first day, added a special sparkle of his own—another friend we must have known for years.

    Johnny—our "Littlest Cowboy" and Kevin our not-so-little-cowboy as comfortable in the saddle as if they were born there—and wished they were.

    Louise—so kind to everyone, anxious, eager to please and hard-working.

    Bud—Thanks for the beer and extra hospitality!

    I tried to soak up enough forests, mountains, meadows, creeks, horses and friendly people to last till next year but I know it definitely takes longer than a week! All of our memories are not condensed here, either, but just a taste.

    Thank you again for a wonderful vacation.

    Warmest Regards,

Sandy Brown

T Cross

P.O. Box 638
Dubois, Wyoming 82513

In 1947, a thirteen-year-old girl from an established eastern family arrived with her parents at the T Cross. Having recently pored over *My Friend Flicka* by Mary O'Hara, she eagerly anticipated spending several weeks glued to the saddle.

The T Cross's owner, Dr. Robert Cox, recognized the young buckerette's passion for horses and handed over to her a young filly to train. This was the beginning of Emily Stevens's escape from the East and lifelong love affair with the West and the T Cross.

Eighteen years later and fed up with Boston, Emily returned to the T Cross to stay. She spent a year as apprentice to Cox, then in 1966, equipped with Cox's high-powered guest and supply lists, she took over the ranch. Emily thrived on gathering the herd at sunrise and spending endless hours on horseback, diving down steep mountain ravines, scaling high ridges, and galloping across sagebrush flats. She knew how to wrangle and saddle, and she knew all the horses' idiosyncrasies.

"My friends back East thought I was crazy," Emily says. Once when the pack rats ate the backs out of thirty-two dining-room chairs, she thought so herself and almost quit the business.

Some twenty years earlier, Cox, a mechanical engineer from MIT, had also escaped the East in search of a western way of life. In Yellowstone he met Charlie Moore, who invited him to work on his CM Ranch in Dubois. "Bob started as a wrangler. Then he met Helen, a beauty of a lady from Wellsley," Emily recalls. "Helen's aunt had offered her a trip either to Europe or out West. She chose the West and that was the end of her."

After two years at the CM, the couple married. When they stumbled upon the T Cross—a 160-acre homestead settled in 1917—they knew it was an ideal spot for a dude ranch. They purchased it for $35,000 and in 1930 opened for business. Nestled at the base of the Absaroka Range and a

Wranglers kept busy during the long, cold winter months building furniture for the T Cross. Today the main lodge looks much the same as it did in the thirties, when this photograph was taken. (Photo courtesy Emily Stevens)

Below: Ken Neal's Uncle Jack and Aunt Bernice Neal, proudly dressed in everyday attire circa 1935. The Neals were managers of one of Jackson Hole's finest dude ranches, the Bear Paw, for eighteen years. They made sure that young Ken enjoyed his summers on the ranch. Little did they know that someday he would follow in their footsteps and become a western host. (Photo by Harrison R. Crandall, courtesy T Cross Ranch)

T Cross Ranch:

(307) 455–2206
Season: Mid-June–
early October
Rates weekly: $875
Special activities:
Pack trips, fly-
fishing
Airport: Jackson Hole
or Riverton
Guest capacity: 24

The T Cross is nestled in a secluded mountain valley near the vast Washakie Wilderness in northwestern Wyoming. Because the ranch is surrounded by miles of national forest, guests enjoy complete privacy and access to terrain which is seldom visited. (Photo courtesy Emily Stevens)

Olivier Lorenceau, from France, whoops it up at the kids' gymkhana. (Photo by Jim Evans)

the end of a rugged dirt road, thirty miles from the small but wild gambling town of Dubois, the place was a gem.

In 1992, Ken and Garey Neal, both experienced wranglers and dude-ranch managers, purchased the T Cross from Emily. "The T Cross is like the ones we worked on as children—the sound of the stream, the isolation," Ken says.

The Neals have made no attempt to change the ranch. The road is still bumpy and most of the cabins are original, with original furnishings and wood-burning stoves for heat. The privies are inside and the cabins have electricity, but there is no television. After a long day riding in the mountains, dudes curl up on comfy, rustic pole beds.

Once inside the T Cross gates, dudes rarely even feel like trekking to town. The serenity of the ranch is intoxicating. (Drawing from an early brochure, courtesy Emily Stevens)

Menu from the T Cross

Menu: Cheese Enchiladas, Corn & Rice Salad, Black Beans

CHEESE ENCHILADAS
Sauce:
1/4 cup olive oil
2 cloves garlic, minced
1 15-ounce can tomato sauce
1 cup water
1/2 cup flour blended with
2 Tbsp. chili powder

Prepare sauce first. Sauté garlic in olive oil. Stir in flour mixture to form thick paste. Whisk in water until smooth. Add tomato sauce.

Filling:
5 cups Monterey Jack cheese, grated, (reserve 1 cup for topping)
2 cups onion, diced
1 1/2 cups diced green chilies
1 cup chopped olives
1 tsp. cumin seed
40 corn tortillas

Mix first five ingredients. Heat tortillas in a 250° oven just until limp enough to roll. Spread a thin layer of sauce in a 9 x 13 baking dish. Roll filling in tortillas and arrange in dish. Cover with sauce and sprinkle remaining cheese over top. Cover with foil. Bake at 350° for 20 minutes.

CORN & RICE SALAD
4 cups long grain white rice
3 lbs. tomatoes, diced
2 red or green bell peppers, diced
1 cup red onion, chopped
4 cups frozen corn kernels, thawed

Cook rice until tender, about 20 minutes. Add remaining ingredients.

Dressing:
1 cup olive oil
1 cup fresh cilantro, chopped
6 Tbsp. white wine vinegar
2 Tbsp. Dijon mustard
2 1/2 tsp. ground cumin
1 tsp. each salt and pepper
1 large fresh jalapeño pepper, minced

Combine above ingredients and pour over salad. Cover and refrigerate until time to serve.

BLACK BEANS
1 #10 can black beans
1 medium onion, chopped
1 Tbsp. cumin seed
1 Tbsp. oregano

Mix ingredients in heavy pot or Dutch oven and heat thoroughly. Serve.

Trail Creek Ranch

P.O. Box 10
WILSON, WYOMING 83014

Above: Wildlife artist Bill Freeman paints in one of his favorite spots at Trail Creek. (Photo by Toni Frissell, courtesy Trail Creek Ranch)

Right: Besides skiing, Betty has always been passionate about taking dudes into the backcountry on horseback. (Photo by Tony Frissell, courtesy Trail Creek Ranch)

Dude ranching in Jackson Hole, Wyoming, has always been distinguished by eccentric, independent characters with a taste for culture and a passion for adventure and the outdoors.

In the 1940s, Betty Woolsey, the former captain of the Olympic Ski Team and the editor of *Ski Illustrated*, purchased a ranch at the base of Teton Pass and moved to the valley. She discovered her ranch while skiing Teton Pass with a friend. At the base of the pass, the two came upon a cabin, where they joined a friendly couple, the Davises, for a cup of coffee. After spending time in the meadows and woods around the cabin and enthusiastically observing beaver, moose, and deer, Betty fell in love with the place.

"I had a curious feeling of being at home here and felt that perhaps someday I would own it," she wrote in her fascinating autobiography, *Off the Beaten Track.*

Soon after that, Betty purchased the Davis place.

Her independent, pioneer spirit mirrored those of the early dude ranchers. As a dude ranch owner, she was in the tradition of people such as Struthers Burt of the Bar BC, a Princeton professor who escaped the East to entertain countesses and Groton graduates in the wild; Lou Joy, of the JY, host to writer Owen Wister; Frank Galey of the White Grass Ranch, a boisterous storyteller loved by all who met him; and Coulter and Margaret Huyler of the Bear Paw, who wined and dined some of the finest clientele. The Hole, a society of roughnecks and tenderfeet, was rustic and civilized—peaceful at times, yet often unruly.

"The ranch started as a house party for friends," says Betty, who invited all her ski buddies out to play. When she moved to the ranch, there were few buildings and no electricity or running water.

Today the primary activity a

Dude Wes Simmons plays cowboy for the summer. (Photo by Toni Frissell, courtesy Trail Creek Ranch)

Trail Creek is riding. Other than half-day or all-day rides through spectacular country, the only other scheduled events are meals. However, guests can keep busy swimming in the heated pool, canoeing or hiking in Grand Teton National Park, or reading a good book in the majestic surroundings of the ranch. Since this is a working ranch, guests are welcome to help with wrangling and bucking hay bales. Pack trips are also available.

In the winter months, guests linger over meals and usually end up curled up on a couch listening to some of Betty's stories. Many guests also enjoy swing dancing at the Stagecoach or famous Million Dollar Cowboy Bar in Jackson Hole.

When asked if dude ranching has changed, Betty is quick to respond. "We played a lot more cards, and in the earlier days it was a pleasure to go downtown and get a milkshake. You could hear yourself talk." But for dudes, Trail Creek is a peaceful escape and a home away from home.

Trail Creek Recipe

END OF THE TRAIL BEANS

2 medium onions, diced
6 strips bacon, diced
3 Tbsp. brown sugar
3 Tbsp. apple cider vinegar
1 Tbsp. dry mustard
3 Tbsp. Worcestershire sauce
2 cloves garlic, minced
1/2 cup ketchup
1 tsp. salt
1 Tbsp. black pepper
1 #10 can pork 'n' beans
1 15-oz. can kidney beans
1 15-oz. can lima beans
1 15-oz. can navy beans

Sauté onion and bacon until onion is transparent. Do not drain fat. Add all ingredients except beans. Let simmer 5–10 minutes. Drain beans and mix together with cooked ingredients in baking dish. Bake at 350° for 1 1/2 hours covered, then cook 15 minutes uncovered. (This dish tastes even better if cooking time is doubled or tripled.)

The classic old barn at Trail Creek, built by Wesley Bircher, provides a focal point for the ranch. (Photo by Toni Frissell, courtesy Trail Creek Ranch)

Inset: Guests still enjoy a weekly gymkhana, where dudes play games on horseback. (Photo by Toni Frissell, courtesy Trail Creek Ranch)

Betty Woolsey, former captain of the Women's Olympic Ski Team, skis untracked powder. (Photo courtesy Trail Creek Ranch)

Triangle X

STAR ROUTE BOX 120
MOOSE, WYOMING 83012

ith the jagged Grand Teton Mountains looming in the distance, the bugling of an elk breaks the morning silence. Nearby, a moose, silhouetted against pastures of sage and cottonwood trees, grazes on willows. Closer to the ranch, a magpie taunts a ranch dog from a corral fence. The morning breakfast bell sounds.

Triangle X was established as a working ranch in 1926 by the John S. Turner family of Utah. In the late twenties, the ranch was purchased by the Rockefeller family, who were buying up land in the Jackson Hole,

Wyoming, area for preservation purposes. Later, when Grand Teton National Park was established, Triangle X was granted permission to continue as a working ranch within the park's boundaries; it is the only dude ranch within the national park system.

Louise Bertschy came to the ranch in 1935, after having met and fallen in love with her guide on an elk-hunting trip, John Turner, the son of John S. Turner. Thus began Louise's love affair with her mountain home and the start of her career as a dude rancher on one of Jackson's most prominent ranches.

When she began at the ranch, she admits she didn't know how to boil water. But she learned how to do everything that needed doing and today acts as hostess and is in charge of activities. When she smiles and invites you to join her for supper, her grace and charm are unparalleled.

She always glows when she recalls the

Right: A cowboy offers to help this dude girl with her tent. (Photo courtesy of the Dude Ranchers Association)

Facing page: Young Louise Bertschy, dressed for a Jackson Hole parade. (Photo by Harrison Crandall)

Triangle X Ranch:

(307) 733–2183
Season: May 20–November 12
Rates weekly: $700–1,000
Special activities: Pack trips,
  white-water trips, fly-fishing
Airport: Jackson Hole
Guest capacity: 70

From the Triangle X Kitchen

RANCH BREAD

2 eggs
4 cups lukewarm water
6 ounces margarine, melted
1 1/2 Tbsp. salt
3/8 cup powdered milk
3/8 cup sugar
3 ounces yeast
6 1/2 lbs. all-purpose flour, or enough to make stiff dough

Put all ingredients except yeast and flour in the large bowl of an electric mixer with a dough hook. At this point, add any herbs or seasonings desired, i.e., garlic, onion, dill, rosemary. Blend well. Add yeast and mix. Gradually add flour, incorporating well after each addition. Dough should be soft but not sticky. Cover and let rise until double. Punch dough down.

On lightly floured surface, form dough into four loaves or into rolls. Place in greased pans or on cookie sheets. Let rise till doubled. Bake in preheated 350° oven for 20 minutes, or till golden. Bread is done when it sounds hollow when tapped. Allow to cool 10 minutes in pans before removing.

Note: Whole wheat or bread flour can be substituted for part of the white flour.

many guests they have had on the ranch. "Half the time you might be sitting next to a really famous person and you don't even know it. All you know is that his name is Jim and he is in such and such a cabin and you talk about this and that and about the ride. Then you pick up *Time* magazine or *Newsweek* and—egads! There's somebody who has been on the ranch last week. I've done it a hundred times."

Louise chuckles as she remembers a successful New York career woman calling off her wedding for one of the Triangle X cowboys. She recalls a young child hugging their oldest and slowest horse, repeating over and over again, "I don't care if you are slow. I love you anyway." And she smiles with pride over one of her dudes calling her after he had purchased a dude ranch and exclaiming, "You never told me this was hard work!"

"A dude ranch is not a hotel or motel. Creating a home is the core of it. . . . We have guests who come back thirty-five years later and say, 'Oh Louise, we are so glad—the ranch is just like we remembered it.' When you have adults crying at the end of their stay, you know you've done your job." Over forty of their guests have since purchased homes in the Jackson area.

Today the ranch is run by Louise, her three sons and their wives, and eight grandchildren. As a family, they love sharing their passion for the country and for ranching with their guests. Louise says, "If this new generation does it right, there will be another golden era of dude ranching. It all depends on the young people. They have to create that feeling of a home—and a feeling of togetherness, which I think people are looking for today with the scattering of families."

For the saddle-sore dude, Triangle X offers a scenic float trip on the Snake River. In the early morning and evening, guests are bound to see moose, elk, deer, buffalo, bald eagle, and beaver. (Photos courtesy Triangle X)

...ve: A string of dudes come back to the
...ch to roost. The Grand Tetons loom in the
...kground. (Photo by Harrison R. Crandall,
...rtesy Teton County Historical Society)

Dudes watch as the cowboys move cattle in for branding. (Photo by
Harrison R. Crandall, Crandall Family collection.)

Left: Nothing tastes better in the wilderness than fresh trout and a
little cowboy coffee. (Photo by Ardean R. Miller III, courtesy of the
Dude Ranchers Association)

Tumbling River Ranch

P.O. BOX 30
GRANT, COLORADO
80448

Tumbling River Ranch dudes cool off in the river. (Photo by Design Den, courtesy Tumbling River Ranch)

The cook is probably the single-most important person on a dude ranch. "Cooks are queer creatures," wrote Struthers Burt in *Diary of a Dude Wrangler.* "Personally, I believe that no man willingly becomes a cook unless he is slightly insane."

Stories from the dude ranches tell of cooks who have quit in the midst of a dinner party for forty, enjoyed one too many drinks on the job, exploded in emotional outburst over the capricious Dutch oven, and in one case on the OTO Ranch in Montana, a Japanese cook insisted on serving cooked lettuce. The same cook pilfered all the rice from the kitchen to make saki in the basement.

Mary Dale and Jim Gordon purchased the Tumbling River Ranch in 1975 from Ernie and Meezie Keys, who had run the place since the early forties. Mary Dale Gordon discovered the unpredictable nature of the cook the first year as a dude rancher, when her cook failed to return for the evening meal and Mary Dale was left to her own devices to prepare dinner for fifty ravenous dudes.

"All of a sudden I had to learn," said Mary Dale. "Somehow I managed." But she learned from then on never to "let the cook have you over the barrel."

"People come to dude ranches to ride horses and eat—and I don't know which

Dudette finds her cowboy. (Photo courtesy Meezie Keyes)

Tumbling River Ranch:

(800) 654–8770

Season: June–August; smaller program August 27–September 30

Rates weekly: June: adults $1,200, under 12 $1,100, under 6 $1,000, under 3 $400; July–August: adults $1,500, under 12 $1,200, under 6, $1,000, under 3 $600

Special activities: Pack trips, white-water trips, fly fishing, swimming pool

Airport: Denver

Guest capacity: 55

After dinner dudes sing, chat, and tell tall tales in front of the fire at the Lost Valley Ranch in Sedalia, Colorado, 1950. At the Tumbling River Ranch once a week, wranglers invite dudes to take the stage and sing, act, play an instrument, or entertain. (Photo courtesy Meezie Keyes)

Tumbling River Ranch guests today learn the cowboy way just like early dudes featured in this Union Pacific photograph did. (Photo courtesy Meezie Keyes)

order," Mary Dale continues. "We wouldn't dream of serving imitation chocolate or fake cheese," Mary Dale says. If the food is good and it rains all day no one complains.

"My philosophy is that in every meal there has to be something exceptional, like green chilies in grilled cheese or an outstanding cookie. You do something people wouldn't do for themselves at home. They can go home and diet." A dude-ranch vacation is not the time to turn down s'mores, buttermilk pancakes, Grandma's coffee cake, popovers, chocolate-chip cheesecake, and juicy barbecued meats.

"In the early days, food was the cause of more worry than perhaps anything else," wrote Struthers Burt. Eggs were particularly scarce.

Burt kept an icehouse full of beef, mutton, pork, ham, bacon, eggs, fruit, and fresh vegetables that could not be grown locally. In addition, fish and game birds caught or shot in season by guests of the ranch had to be stored. And a milk house kept dairy products cold. Under the best conditions, other ranch storehouses were stocked with duplicate supplies so that any item could be replenished immediately.

Today Tumbling River Ranch still maintains the western atmosphere of the early ranch. For Mary Dale and Jim, the most important part of their business is making sure families enjoy their stay. While the riding, campfires, talent shows, swimming, and sightseeing bring much joy, it is the thought that people are eating well and enjoying conversation that gives Mary Dale the most pleasure.

This photograph circa 1940 was taken by the Union Pacific Railroad as a promotional shot for Colorado dude ranching. (Photo courtesy Meezie Keyes)

From Mary Dale's Kitchen

POTATO CHILI CHEESE SOUP

4 medium potatoes, peeled, diced
3 cups water
1 Tbsp. butter
1 Tbsp. olive oil
1 1/2 cups diced onion
1 1/2 tsp. salt
1 tsp cumin
1 tsp basil
2 cloves garlic, minced
1/2 tsp pepper
1 1/2 cups diced green pepper
1 cup diced green chilies
3/4 cup sour cream
1 cup milk
3/4 cup grated Monterey Jack

Boil potatoes in water until tender. Mash them right in the water until smooth. In the butter and the oil, sauté the onions, salt, cumin, basil, garlic, and pepper until the onions are tender. Add the green peppers and the green chilies and saute for five more minutes. Add the vegetables to the potatoes. Then, add sour cream, milk, and Monterey Jack cheese. Heat through without boiling. (We use our leftover mashed potatoes in this soup. Just combine the potatoes and hot water until soup is at the desired thickness.) Serves 8.

(Photo by Charles J. Belden, courtesy The Belden Museum, Meeteetse, WY)